Roots and Wings

A Comedy

Frank Vickery

A SAMUEL FRENCH ACTING EDITION

SAMUEL FRENCH

FOUNDED 1830

SAMUELFRENCH-LONDON.CO.UK
SAMUELFRENCH.COM

FOR AMATEUR PRODUCTION ENQUIRIES

UNITED KINGDOM AND WORLD EXCLUDING NORTH AMERICA

plays@SamuelFrench-London.co.uk

020 7255 4302/01

Each title is subject to availability from Samuel French,

depending upon country of performance.

ROOTS AND WINGS

First performed at the Sherman Theatre, Cardiff, on May
18th, 1995 with the following cast:

Ruby	Menna Trussler
Griff	Hubert Rees
Nurse	Lorraine Cole
Nigel	Greg Ashton
Vernon	Dafydd Hywel
Rita	Sue Roderick

Directed by Phil Clark
Designed by Jonathan Fensom
Lighting designed by Keith Hemming

CHARACTERS

Ruby: mid-fifties
Griff: Ruby's husband; mid-fifties
Nurse: youngish
Nigel: Ruby's and Griff's son; mid- to late twenties
Vernon: mid-forties
Rita: Vernon's wife; mid-forties

The play takes place in a corridor, and inside a small hospital room

Time: the present

SYNOPSIS OF SCENES

ACT I
SCENE 1   Hospital corridor. 9.45 a.m.
SCENE 2   Hospital room. 9.45 a.m.

ACT 2
The corridor and room combined. 10.15 a.m.

Other plays by Frank Vickery
published by Samuel French Ltd

Full length:
All's Fair
Biting the Bullet
Breaking the String
Easy Terms
Erogenous Zones
Family Planning
A Kiss on the Bottom
Loose Ends
Love Forty
A Night on the Tiles
One O'Clock from the House
Spanish Lies
Trivial Pursuits

One act:
After I'm Gone
Green Favours
A Night Out
Split Ends

ACT I
Scene 1

A hospital corridor. 9.45 a.m.

We are facing across the corridor. c *of the back wall is a set of red double doors with windows in them. There are two chairs set against the wall* l, *two chairs similarly and a coffee machine* r

Traffic noise is heard as the audience are entering the auditorium

The house Lights fade to Black-out. As they do so, one almighty crash — the sound of a car crash — is heard

The stage Lights come up to reveal Ruby sitting in a chair l *of the double doors*

Ruby is a woman in her mid-fifties. She is wearing the uniform — including hat — of a lollipop lady and has a shopping bag on her lap. She has a large white man's handkerchief in her hand and is wiping her nose with it. After a moment, she gets up and peers through the door windows into the room beyond

Nurse (*female; off*) I'll be back in a minute.

Ruby steps back to let the Nurse through

The Nurse comes out of the room carrying a tray covered by a white cloth. She has a stethoscope around her neck

Ruby Is that it? Can I go in now, nurse?
Nurse (*shaking her head*) Not quite finished with him yet. Shouldn't be long though.
Ruby How is he this morning?
Nurse A definite improvement on yesterday, I'd say. (*She pauses slightly before making to leave* l)
Ruby I heard somebody laughing just now. Was it him?
Nurse No, it was me. He's a real live wire once he starts, isn't he?

Ruby He's a hell of a boy, mind. He's never happy unless he's making people laugh. (*She laughs*)

Nurse (*making to leave; smiling*) Ten minutes and he'll be ready for his audience.

Ruby puts her hand on the Nurse's arm, stopping her

Ruby Good God, he's told you as well, has he?

Nurse (*after a slight pause*) Sorry?

Ruby Still, that's the best way to be, I suppose. I keep telling Griff — that's my husband — "Things will be much better now it's all out in the open," I said. Griff's only just recently found out. I've known for a while. It's not so bad when you've had time to get used to the idea, see, is it?

Nurse (*suddenly realizing what Ruby is on about; smiling*) I won't be long.

The Nurse exits

Ruby sits in the chair again, but after a second or two she gets up and looks into the room. She can't really see anything so she sits back down. She takes a box of "Roses" chocolates out of her bag, opens it and eats one. She then takes off her hat and puts it in her bag along with the chocolates. There is a pause as she eats the chocolate

Griff enters R. He's about the same age as Ruby. He is carrying his tucker-bag and is wearing his British Rail guard's uniform complete with hat

Ruby looks up and sees Griff

Ruby (*going to him*) Oh, Griff. You came after all.

Griff Let's get this straight now before we start, right? I'm not here for him — it's you I've come for.

Ruby You can't say that, he's our son.

Griff He might be your son, Ruby, but I told him Saturday night, if he was going to carry on with all that nonsense he'd be no son of mine. I meant it then and, accident or no, I mean it now.

Ruby takes Griff by the arm and walks him downstage c

Ruby Don't talk like that — he might never come out of here!

Griff (*moving away R and putting his bag down on the chair next to the coffee machine*) He's got a couple of bruises, a few cracked ribs and a knock on the head. He's not going to die, Ruby. He'll be out of this place by Thursday — you take it from me.

Ruby (*following Griff*) Look here, he didn't come round hardly at all yesterday and he talked a heap of nonsense for a solid hour last night.

Griff He's been talking nonsense since last Saturday if you ask me.

Ruby Well, I'm not asking you and I told you this morning, you've got to forget last Saturday.

Griff I can't.

Ruby Well, you're going to have to. (*She moves back to her seat and sits*) For the moment, anyway.

Griff (*sitting on the chair next to his tucker-bag*) It's like a bloody nightmare. It keeps playing over and over in my head.

Ruby (*after a slight pause*) There's no way he'll be out of here this weekend. He's in no fit state. (*She has a thought*) They're hiding something from me, I'm sure they are.

Griff Don't talk rubbish.

Ruby They are, I can tell.

Griff They've said he's all right.

Ruby Yes, but they're not going to tell me everything, are they? And you must be concerned as well if the truth be known, because nothing could shift you to come here with me this morning. (*She has an idea and stands*) They haven't sent for you, have they?

Griff No.

Ruby You're sure now, they haven't rung to tell you to come here?

Griff Would I be dressed for the afternoon shift if there was anything wrong?

Ruby Tell me why you changed your mind, then?

Griff For you. I changed it for you. I didn't want you to be on your own.

There is a slight pause. Ruby sits back down on her usual chair. Griff takes a pack of sandwiches out of his bag

Ruby There was a policeman here earlier on confirming there was no other car involved.

Griff So what do they think happened then?

Ruby They *know* what happened. He fell asleep at the wheel.

Griff Well, I'm not surprised — should never be doing two jobs. I don't know anyone who can survive on three or four hours' sleep.

Ruby Yes, he has been overdoing it lately.

Griff Sandwich?

Ruby Good God no, I can't eat *now*.

There is a pause. Ruby takes another chocolate out of the box and eats it

Griff (*eating*) When he gets out of here later this week, perhaps you'd better suggest him giving up that "club" lark.

Ruby I'm not suggesting anything of the sort.

Griff Well, he's hardly going to listen to me, is he?

Ruby You still don't get it, do you, Griff? (*She moves to him*) If Nigel decides, for whatever reason, to give up one of his jobs, it'll be his day job in Cardiff. It's not going to be the clubs, you can bet your bottom dollar on that.

Griff Let's be honest, you wouldn't talk him out of doing it anyway, even if he *would* listen to you.

Ruby No, you're right, I wouldn't.

Griff God, you must be as proud as he is.

Ruby (*moving down* L) I am. He's damned good at what he does and you thought so too till you realized who he was.

Griff (*looking at Ruby*) Yes, and I'll never forgive him for that — or you either.

Ruby How else was the boy supposed to tell you?

Griff Like any other normal person.

Ruby Griff, if he was normal, there'd be nothing to tell.

Griff Am I that bad a father that I couldn't be told in the privacy of my own house?

Ruby In a word, yes. (*She moves to him again*) You know what you were like when he wouldn't take that job with you on the railway.

Griff That was a damned good job, that was.

Ruby (*moving away again*) Yes, I know it was — but he didn't want it, did he?

Griff No, he'd rather go and dress windows in Cardiff. The writing was on the wall then. (*A slight pause*) Well, that's it as far as the club is concerned, you know that, don't you?

Ruby What do you mean?

Griff We're home every Saturday night from now on because there's no way I can show my face in that place again.

Ruby Oh, for goodness' sake, what's the matter with you? Anyone would think he robbed a bank or committed murder or something.

Griff I think I could cope better with it if he had.

Ruby (*firmly*) Look, it's not easy for me either, mind.

Griff I was the butt of all the jokes in work yesterday.

Ruby Well, that's just great that is, isn't it? There they all were in the club Saturday night ——

Griff Exactly ——

Ruby — all your work mates having a marvellous time, and today? Today they mock him for it.

Griff It's not Nigel they were mocking, it was me.

Ruby You think you're by yourself in that? I get it too, mind. I get in supermarkets, in bus queues, I get it when I stop the cars to let the children cross the road. It happened last week. The car window was down and I heard this woman say, (*she turns and faces down* L) "See her by there? Her son dresses up in women's clothes." I waited till the last child was across the road and I stood right in front of her car. "My son is a female impersonator," I said. "He does it for a living. I heard your husband does it for kicks!" With that, the car revved up and if I hadn't jumped to one side ... (*she jumps* L) I swear to God, she'd have run me over.

There is a pause. Ruby sits back down on her chair

Griff It sounds like everyone knew except me.
Ruby He tried to tell you.
Griff So when did you find out? (*He stares at Ruby during the following*)
Ruby Well, I was in his bedroom one day, dusting — and he'd left the wardrobe door open. (*A small smile spreads across her face as she remembers — then she becomes aware of Griff's gaze and the smile is quickly removed*) When I asked him about it, he told me.
Griff He'd have told you eventually, anyway. You've always been close and that's half the trouble.

Ruby looks at Griff

Don't look like that, it's true. Me and him ... we've never had anything going for us. He's embarrassed me all his life.
Ruby (*returning to her chair*) The trouble with you is you've got a short memory. You want to think back to last Saturday in the club.
Griff I don't have to think back to it — I can't get the bloody thing out of my brain.
Ruby You were having a marvellous time.
Griff And that's what hurts the most.
Ruby (*after a slight pause*) Tell me why you like the drag acts, Griff?
Griff I don't know ... they're a bit of fun, I suppose.
Ruby Exactly. You thought "The Dolly Sisters" were the best act the club had booked in months. You were killing yourself laughing. I know because I watched you. You laughed so much I thought you weren't going to stop.
Griff (*standing and moving down* R) And the fact is I haven't laughed once since.
Ruby They were marvellous, Nigel and his friend — everybody loved them, they were so professional. All right, maybe it was a bit cruel to call you up on the stage with them, but you were glad to go at the time. You were having a ball — till Nigel took his wig off.
Griff I wanted to die.
Ruby I swear to God, I didn't know he was going to do that. And in fairness,

I don't think he'd planned it either. I think he just seized the moment when he could.

Griff (*quietly*) I just wanted to crawl in a corner and die.

Ruby You hid your feelings pretty well then.

Griff No, I didn't. (*After a slight pause*) When I wiped my eyes everyone thought, including you, it was because I was laughing so much and it was — until I realized it was my boy up there. (*A slight pause. He sits back down*) You can't imagine how I felt.

Ruby Of course I can.

Griff No, you can't. It's different for a father.

Ruby (*moving to him*) In what way?

Griff I can't explain it.

Ruby Try.

Griff I felt so ...

Ruby Disappointed?

Griff (*trying to find the words*) Cheated.

Ruby Even after all the laughter?

Griff *Because* of all the laughter.

Ruby You're saying you'd have taken it better if they didn't like him so much?

Griff It would have been a lot less embarrassing for me, yes.

Ruby So you'd have rather he had died up on that stage then, would you?

Griff Yes.

Ruby (*shouting*) Is that what you're saying?

Griff (*shouting*) Yes!

Ruby (*after a slight pause during which she moves down* L) Nigel hasn't done anything that you haven't done in the past.

Griff What are you talking about?

Ruby You've dressed up as a woman before now.

Griff I have not!

Ruby What about the Blackpool trip then? I can still remember you now, prancing up and down the aisle of that bus wearing my green lurex dress and Mary Morgan's false hairpiece. I'm sure Nigel can remember you as well. There's a photo of you too, somewhere.

Griff That was only a bit of fun.

Ruby And last Saturday night wasn't?

Griff That's a different thing altogether.

Ruby No, it's not. The only difference is that you entertained forty people on a bus and he entertained four hundred down the club.

Griff No, no — you can say what you like, there's a lot more to it than that.

Ruby Tell me why you did it then, Griff?

Griff (*after a slight pause*) I don't know — I was probably drunk.

Ruby Come on — you can do better than that.

Griff I can't remember.

Ruby Well I can.

Griff Then why the hell do you want me to tell you?

Ruby I want to hear you say it. (*A slight pause*) OK, I'll help you out. You always saw yourself as a bit of a lad, didn't you? Hard to imagine looking at you now, but you like attention, Griff. Nigel follows you for that. That's why you were quite happy to join the drag act up on the stage. You like making people laugh. The trouble is you think that last Saturday the joke was on you.

Griff It was.

Ruby Then it was on me, too.

Griff No, it wasn't. You knew who you were looking at. You knew why you were laughing.

Ruby (*sitting next to Griff*) I wasn't laughing at you, Griff, and neither was anyone else.

Griff They might not have laughed at me at the time but they've laughed at me enough since. I'm the talk of the place. We all are. (*A slight pause*) I shouldn't have found out the way I did.

Ruby No, I know, love, I know. (*She puts her hand on his leg*) Only last week I said to him, "You'd better tell your father quick," I said. "You take that booking at the club and he's bound to find out sooner or later."(*A slight pause*) I think the plan was to tell you after his spot, or later on when we got home, but you were enjoying yourself so much at the time ...

Griff Do you think he's ... (*A slight pause*) He is, isn't he?

Ruby What?

Griff You know what I mean.

They look at each other for a brief moment

Ruby Well ... they say it doesn't go hand in hand, you know, but ... yes, he is. (*A slight pause, during which she stands and moves down* L) Do you know what hurts me the most? Oh, not that he'll never get married ... but that I'll never show a little grandchild of mine across the road and into school. (*A slight pause*) And then I thought, well there's nothing I can do about it, you can't have the penny and the bun, can you? I'm going to have to settle for the fact that my son is a cabaret artist ... and a very good one at that.

Griff I wish it was that easy for me.

Ruby It's not a question of it being easy, Griff. Our hands are tied. We play the game with the cards we're dealt. We either accept him for what he is or we don't. (*A slight pause*) Do you know how he told me?

Griff shakes his head

Do you want to know?

He nods

I suppose it was about two years ago now. (*She returns to her chair*) It was a Saturday morning and you were in work. I knew there was something up, he was hanging around my feet, you know generally getting in the way. In the end I said, "Come on, what is it? If you've got something on your mind, spit it out." He was at the table and he told me to sit down, so I did. The whole atmosphere changed. The sparkle went from his eyes and he came over all serious. I didn't like it at all. "Hey, what is it?" I said. "You're frightening me now." He held his arms out across the table and grabbed me by the hands so tight I could see the whites of his knuckles. He looked me straight in the eye. "I've got a brain tumour", he said, "and I've only got three months to live." Oh my God, I could feel myself floating off. Then he yanked my hands and it suddenly brought me back. "No, I haven't," he said. "It's all right, I'm not going to die. I'm only gay." I could have bloody killed him ... it's a funny old world though, isn't it, 'cause I kissed him instead.

There is a pause

The Nurse returns

Nurse (*seeing Griff*) Oh, Mr Gregory. Nigel asked me if you were here. I'll tell him.
Griff (*getting up*) Er, no ... I'm not staying.
Nurse Oh, can't you pop your head round, I'm not going to be much longer.
Griff I've got to get to work.
Nurse All right — go on, nip in now, then, if you want to.
Griff (*shouting*) No, I said! You bloody deaf or what?

The Nurse looks at Ruby then exits through the double doors into the room

There is a pause

Griff turns to leave

Ruby (*shouting after him*) You're going to be a lonely old man, Griff.
Griff (*turning immediately*) You never tried, not once, not once when he was growing up, to interest him in ——
Ruby (*moving to Griff*) Hey, you can't blame me. Now it's not my fault. That's the first thing Nigel said to me. He said, "Now look, Mam", he said, "you mustn't blame yourself", and I don't. How he's turned out has got nothing to do with me at all.

Griff You saying it's *my* fault?

Ruby You're the one who dressed up and entertained them on the bus. Who's to say what put the idea into his head?

Griff (*after a slight pause*) You don't think it was that, do you?

Ruby No, Griff. You didn't make him what he is and neither did I.

Griff Well, we must have done something.

Ruby All I've done is to accept him for what he is because he's my son and I love him.

Griff I can't think like that.

Ruby You still love him, don't you?

Griff doesn't answer

> (*Moving away down* L) If you don't feel the same as me then I feel sorry because you're going to miss out on something very special.

Griff Special?

Ruby Yes, special. (*She turns to face Griff*) You're a hypocrite, Griff Gregory, and not a very nice one at that.

Griff Is there any other kind?

Ruby (*a thought strikes her*) It's Monday. Did you remember to put the rubbish out?

Griff Have I ever forgot?

Ruby (*after a slight pause*) Everything will be all right in the end.

Griff looks at Ruby

> (*Moving to Griff*) We've still got him — that's all that matters. We could have lost him in that crash. How would you have felt then?

Griff A lot like I do now, I suppose.

Ruby Look, when you go in there and you see him ——

Griff I'm not going in there. I told you when I came here it was only for you.

Ruby I'm sure he'd *like* to see you.

Griff Well, we can't all have what we like.

Ruby Refusing to see him isn't going to make it better.

Griff And going in there is?

Ruby It's not going to make it any worse.

Griff I can't go in there. I can't look him in the face.

Ruby Why, it's the same face you looked at last week.

Griff It's the same face I looked at last Saturday — minus the make-up.

Ruby And the wig. Don't forget the wig. (*She laughs*)

Griff It's not funny.

Ruby Of course it is; it's bloody hysterical. We'll all be laughing about it now in a couple of months.

Griff I should have put my foot down. I knew the way things were going right from early on. (*A slight pause*) And then when he went off to London, well, that was good enough. I saw it coming. I should have done something — took him to football matches and —

Ruby Oh, for goodness' sake, Griff, what's the matter with you? You don't honestly think that watching twenty-two men kick a ball around would have made any difference? You don't live in the real world, you don't. Buying him an Indian outfit for Christmas when he was small instead of a Post Office set wouldn't have changed anything. Good God, even I know that. (*A slight pause*) Look, you're doing what I first did, you're blaming yourself and you shouldn't. You're looking for a reason and there isn't one.

Griff There's got to be.

Ruby (*returning to her seat*) Well, there's not.

Griff What went wrong then? Tell me, I need to know because something somewhere went wrong. (*He follows her*) There must have been a time when he realized he was what he was. I mean, you don't just wake up one day and choose to be something like that, and if it's got nothing to do with you or me and the way he was brought up, then what has it got to do with? Where's the reason for it? I don't believe it when you say there isn't one. (*He turns away slightly*) Why didn't he tell us about it at the time, maybe he could have had help, we could have taken him to see somebody who could have talked to him, somebody who could have listened to him and then all this could have been avoided. (*A thought hits him*) Maybe it's not too late. He could go private. We can pay. I bet it would only take a few sessions with someone who knew what they were doing, someone recommended who could get to the heart of his trouble straight away. I don't think it's as big a problem as it first looks, it's only a question of preference, isn't it? So it shouldn't be difficult to find someone who could straighten him out. Get him to see it's only a matter of choice and once all that's sorted, I'm sure the other thing, the dressing-up thing will right itself. What do you think?

Ruby (*after a slight pause*) I don't know much about it, Griff. I suppose there are books you can get on it but I'm sure as hell not going into the library to find out. All I know are the few bits and pieces Nigel has told me. From what I can gather it's not a life-threatening disease, well apart from this AIDS thing. And I know it's not something you can go and have "straightened out" either. It's not like having a tooth pulled and then there you are, that's it, everything's back to normal. (*A slight pause*) If it's only a matter of preference, like you say, is it really that big a deal that he prefers something else? I know it's disappointing and I know it's not what we want, but we don't have a choice, and although you'll find this hard to believe, I don't think Nigel got much say in it either. You don't choose to be different, do you? You just are.

There is a slight pause. Griff sits UR

Griff I can't understand how it's all so "matter of fact" with you.
Ruby Oh, don't think it didn't break my heart because it did. I've lost count
of how many nights I cried myself to sleep. And what made it harder for
me was I couldn't show him or you. (*She moves to him*) I had to cry on my
own and carry on as if nothing had happened when all my world was
collapsing around me. (*A slight pause*) "I'm glad I told you," he said. "It's
like taking a big weight off my chest." Trouble was he took it off his chest
and put it on mine. I'm not complaining, you know — that's what mothers
are for. (*A slight pause*) Do you know what did help me, though?

He doesn't answer

I picked up my magazine one week and some mother had written in that
her son was going through the same sort of thing and do you know what
the advice was?

He still doesn't answer

(*Moving down* L) I can't remember it word for word but it went something
like: "There are two things parents should give their children. Roots and
wings." Roots and wings, Griff. Our Nigel knows there's always a room
for him at home and ——
Griff (*getting up and joining her*) Does that mean he's coming to us when
he gets out of here?
Ruby I don't know, I haven't talked to him about it yet but I hope so. (*A slight
pause*) Whatever he wants to do, Griff, or wherever he wants to fly — it's
OK with me. I'm behind him all the way. All I want is for him to be happy
and there's nothing I wouldn't do to make sure he is.
Griff What if I said he can't come home?
Ruby What if I said you can bugger off?
Griff He's left home, it's not fair to encourage him back.
Ruby What's fair got to do with it? He'll need to recuperate. Kevin won't
be able to do it now that's for sure.
Griff Who the hell is Kevin?
Ruby (*after a slight pause*) Er ... Nigel's friend. The other half of the act.
Griff (*after a slight pause*) Wait a minute. You're not going to tell me that
they live together, are you?
Ruby Well, I was going to, but it's a bit pointless now, isn't it?
Griff I don't believe this.
Ruby You're going to have to learn to be more tolerant, Griff. Shouldn't be
difficult, you've always said, "Live and let live".
Griff Yes, but not when it's your own flesh and blood.

Ruby It should apply even more then.

Griff (*after a slight pause*) So — my son lives with another man. Is there anything else I should know?

Ruby (*moving away* L *slightly*) No. I think that's everything.

Griff You sure now? You're not keeping anything back to prevent me having a heart attack?

Ruby Well, there is the little one they're expecting in June, but apart from that there's nothing.

Griff I wish I could joke about it.

Ruby Who says I'm joking?

Griff (*looking at Ruby incredulously*) You're not serious? You are serious, aren't you?

Ruby Look, Kevin used to be married, right? Wife not up to much from what I can gather. I don't know what her job is. I think it's to do with the military though because I heard Kevin say something about her being (*she pronounces the spelling*) R.A.F.

Griff Where's all this leading?

Ruby Well, they had a little girl together. Now the wife has picked up with somebody else and he hasn't taken to the girl, poor little thing. There's a lot of talk of her coming to live with Kevin.

Griff In Nigel's house?

Ruby Well, where else?

Griff (*after a slight pause*) If I don't take in all that's happening, you'll have to appreciate it's because things are moving a bit too fast for me.

Ruby Too fast?

Griff Last week I thought I had an average twenty-five year old son who lived alone and had a mortgage. (*He moves down* L) Today he's a drag queen who shares a house and bed with a man who's already been married and whose daughter is about to move in. I mean there's only so much a guard with British Rail can grasp.

Ruby Oh, I don't know, I think you've grasped it all pretty well, Griff.

Griff (*shouting*) Will you tell me what the hell's happening to us?

Ruby (*shouting back*) Will you keep your voice down? You're in a hospital, remember?

Griff I don't care where I am! Up till last Saturday our family was quite ... (*he searches for the word*) ... orthodox.

Ruby Orthodox? Good God, Griff, you can call us a lot of things but we've hardly been that.

Griff On the surface we were. Now all of a sudden everything's a mess. A mess.

Ruby No, it's not.

Griff (*shouting*) If people make fun of our son, it's a mess! If you get talked about by women in cars, it's a mess! If my workmates take the piss, believe me, it's a bloody mess!

Ruby You shouldn't care what people say.

Griff But I do! It matters when they crack a joke and I can't laugh because we're the butt of it.

Ruby I don't suppose we get a half of the flak that Nigel does. If he can take the slings and arrows, why can't we? If we stick together as a family, Griff, no-one can hurt us.

Griff You don't know what it's like for me. What it was like for me on Saturday night.

Ruby All right, I'll admit it, finding out the way you did that Nigel was a drag artist perhaps came as a bit of a shock to you — but you've got to come to terms with it like I did.

Griff It's not as easy for me.

Ruby I wish you wouldn't keep saying it's not easy for you.

Griff (*insisting*) Well, it's not!

Ruby Well it should be.

Griff Why?

Ruby Well ... you're normal enough *now*.

Griff What do you mean?

Ruby There was a time when we were courting when I used to wonder which side of the fence *you* were going to fall.

Griff You're all right, are you?

Ruby I mean, everybody has a mate, you know, I understand that — but you couldn't move without that Ritchie Thomas. Talk about Tweedledum and Tweedledee. He was like your shadow till I put my foot down.

Griff There was nothing funny about me and Ritchie. We were like brothers, we were.

Ruby You don't take your brother on honeymoon with you.

Griff (*shouting*) I didn't take him on honeymoon.

Ruby (*shouting back*) It's a hell of a coincidence that he ended up in the caravan next to us then, don't you think?

Griff It's not fair to throw Ritchie up. Specially now he's not here to defend himself.

Ruby I'd have said exactly the same if he was alive.

Griff You're a dangerous woman, you are, Ruby.

Ruby I put it all behind me and didn't think much more about it, but after the fool you made of yourself at his funeral it brought it all back.

Griff How many times have I got to tell you, there was never anything like that between us.

Ruby (*quietly*) Funny how he never got married, then.

Griff You want to know why he never got married?

Ruby Go on, surprise me.

Griff I will. He loved somebody who was already married and it wasn't me — it was you. (*A slight pause*) Well ... what do you say to that?

Ruby I knew. (*A slight pause*) Now what do *you* say?

Griff is speechless. There is a slight pause

The Nurse enters from Nigel's room

Nurse There we are then, he's all done and sitting up in bed waiting for you.
(*She makes to go*)
Griff Er ... nurse ...

The Nurse turns round

Just now ... um ... (*He finds it hard to apologize*) What it was ... um ...
Nurse It's all right, forget it.
Ruby No! It's not all right, is it, Griff?
Griff I shouldn't have ... you know, shouted — er — like that. You all do
a good job ... deserve better ...
Ruby He's apologizing but as you see it doesn't come easy.
Griff Does he know I'm here? Nigel?
Nurse I would think the whole ward knows.
Ruby I told you to keep your voice down.
Nurse (*nodding towards Nigel's room*) It's no big deal, you know. You can
change your mind and go in if you want to. (*A slight pause*) Anyway, I've
got to go. (*She smiles*)

The Nurse exits

Ruby (*after a slight pause*) Ritchie Thomas came to see me in a hell of a state
one day.

Griff looks at her

He told me how he felt about me ... *I* told him how he felt about you and
the poor bugger went home in a worst state than when he came in ... (*A slight
pause*) I don't believe for a minute you ever got involved, but — you can't
deny you didn't know how he felt about you.
Griff We grew up together.
Ruby All right, so as far as you were concerned you were close. But he had
feelings for you ——
Griff And you ——
Ruby — that he shouldn't have had and you knew it. You accepted it. Why
can't you do the same for your son?
Griff It's different when it's your own. And anyway, Ritchie never dressed
up in women's clothes, or wanted to as far as I know.
Ruby Good God, Griff, that's only a bit of fun — you've said that yourself.
Griff I can take a joke and have a laugh as good as the next man, but you've
got to admit what our Nigel's into goes a hell of a lot deeper than that.

Ruby All right, so he does take it a bit more serious. He's got to. It's his job. There's nothing more to it than that. At the end of the day all the dresses get put away in a wardrobe.

Griff Who said?

Ruby Hell's delight, do you think he walks round the house in a dress, do you?

Griff It's possible. Who's to say he isn't sitting in there now waiting for us dressed up in a sister's uniform?

Ruby (*laughing*) Good, you're making a joke of it. I'm glad.

Griff I'm dead bloody serious.

Ruby Would it be so awful if he was?

Griff doesn't answer

It shouldn't matter to us if he wanted to go around naked with a frying pan on his head.

Griff You can say what you like, I can't like him for what he does.

Ruby All right, don't — you can still love him for what he is.

Griff You mean in spite of what he is.

Ruby Whatever. Nobody really cares what he does behind his own front door, Griff, and if they do, why should it matter to us?

Griff (*after a slight pause*) You're very good at all this, aren't you? Much better than me.

Ruby I've had more time, love. It'll get easier, I promise.

Griff But it'll never go away.

Ruby No, Griff — it'll never go away. (A *slight pause*) Can I ask you something?

Griff looks at Ruby

Which is the worst for you? The humiliation of Saturday night or the knowledge that your only son is gay?

Griff (*shouting*) It's not fair!

Ruby Of course it's not, but life never is. I want to know what the hardest thing is for you. See, if it's the fact that he's gay, well there's nothing anybody, including Nigel, can do about that. If, on the other hand, it's the drag thing, well ... asking him to give up the dresses isn't going to change him either.

A pause

Griff Do you know what I've gone and done?

Ruby Surprise me.

Griff You know you brought Nigel's suitcases home with you after the accident? The suitcases with all the costumes. (A *slight pause*) I've emptied them. I emptied them into two big plastic bags and put them out with the rubbish this morning.

Ruby Oh my God, and you thought that would solve everything, I suppose?

Griff I don't know what I thought. (*A slight pause*) After Saturday maybe I just wanted to get my own back.

Ruby There was over two thousand pounds worth of frocks in those cases. Not to mention the make-up and wigs.

Griff What can I say?

Ruby Well, nothing to me. I'd start thinking about how you're going to tell Nigel if I were you.

Griff I don't know if I can apologize to him.

Ruby And you won't know unless you try. Anyway, seems to me there's apologies due all round. Go in and see him, go on.

Griff You don't know what you're asking.

Ruby I'm not asking any more of you than I've asked of myself. (*A slight pause*) And you still haven't answered my question.

Griff (*after a slight pause; crossing in front of Ruby*) Going round the clubs like he does — it's like having a tattoo on his forehead.

Ruby So it's not the fact that he's gay then, it's the drag factor?

Griff Why has everyone got to know?

Ruby You'd feel better if he tried to hide it?

Griff I'd feel better if he didn't flaunt it.

Ruby That's what he gets paid for. (*A slight pause*) So it *is* the drag factor.

Griff I'm never going to be able to accept it like you.

Ruby There's only one way to accept it, Griff, and that's a little bit at a time. The first thing to do is to walk in through that door, the second is to smile, and if he smiles back, which he will ... everything will be plain sailing after that.

Griff How can I smile when all I want to do is knock seven different shades of shit out of him?

Ruby Oh, you'll smile, Griff. We both will because the chips are down and we can't do anything else. (*A slight pause*) Do you know, when he was a little boy, all I wished was for him to be happy — and he is. Trouble was, I forgot to wish for me to be happy too.

Griff (*moving to Ruby*) We can walk away, let him get on with it.

Ruby I can't do that, he's my son, he needs me.

Griff (*stopping*) Oh well, there you are then: as long as he's got you.

Ruby And I need him. And although it's not easy for you to admit, you need him too.

Griff (*after a pause: quietly*) Does he need me, do you think?

Ruby The answer is staring you in the face, Griff. It wasn't me he asked the nurse about, it was you.

Griff He only wants me to condone what he's doing.

Ruby He's not after your blessing. He needs you to accept him for what he is, that's not the same thing.

Griff What about what I need?

Ruby Shouldn't come into it. Roots and wings, Griff — remember, roots and wings. (*A slight pause*) You can walk away now if you want to but it's not going to solve anything. Whether you like it or not, you're going to be his father for a long time to come. (*A slight pause*) Closing your eyes isn't going to make him disappear. (*A slight pause*) I'm going in — I bet he's wondering what the hell's going on. (*She heads for the doors*)

Griff Do you want me to come with you?

Ruby (*stopping short of them*) Of course I do: but there's no way I'm going to let you. (*She turns to him*) Not *with* me. You go in there, you go in on your own. (*A slight pause*) Well what's it to be, Griff? Is it time to take your head out of the sand or what? (*A slight pause. She walks towards Griff*) Come on, it can't be as bad as all that. One small step for Griff, one giant leap for Nigel. (*A slight pause*) If it makes you feel any better you'll be killing two birds with one stone.

Griff looks at Ruby

You remember that weight we talked about? You know, the one Nigel took off his chest and put on mine? You can't take it away, I know that, but I'd sleep a hell of a lot easier if you took half. Isn't that what husbands are for?

Griff And sons?

Ruby (*after a slight pause*) Kids. They're all the same: armache when they're small — heartache when grown.

They share a moment. They are almost close

Oh, Griff!

Ruby turns and goes into Nigel's room as if she has given up on Griff

Ruby (*off*) There you are! Oooh you're looking much better today. How are you feeling, all right?

Griff stands motionless for a moment. Slowly he turns to look towards Nigel's room. After he has stared for a moment or two the Lights fade to Black-out

Shirley Bassey is heard singing, "As Long As He Needs Me"

SCENE 2

Inside Nigel's hospital room. 9.45 a.m.

The double doors from the corridor are blue on this side

There is one hospital bed in the room, surrounded by the usual hospital paraphernalia, including a bedside cabinet, and a chair R. There is a window to one side

The music fades and the Lights come up. Nigel is in bed, having his blood pressure taken by the Nurse. He has a dressing on his forehead. Vernon is standing with his back towards the others, looking out of the room window

Nigel ... so there I was sitting in my dressing-room quietly putting on my make-up when this bloody big butch committee man stomped in and said, "Hey, are you bent?" "Why", I said, "have you got a crooked arse?"
Nurse (*laughing*) Don't you ever stop?

Nigel is about to say something again but before he has the chance, the Nurse pops a thermometer into his mouth. She continues to check his blood pressure. Vernon looks over his shoulder at the others before returning to the window

Nurse It's coming down nicely.
Nigel (*taking the thermometer out of his mouth*) Said the actress to the ——
Nurse (*snatching the thermometer out of Nigel's hand*) You're incorrigible, you know that.

The Nurse smiles and pokes the thermometer back through Nigel's lips

Nigel (*with the thermometer still in his mouth*) Don't you like my jokes?
Nurse I love them, but first thing in the morning?
Nigel It's very nice first thing in the morning.
Nurse (*covering a smile*) What is?
Nigel Laughing of course, what else?

There is a pause

Is my father out there?
Nurse Oh ... I thought ... (*She looks over at Vernon*)
Nigel No, that's Vernon. My father-in-law.

Vernon looks and half smiles at the Nurse

Nurse Are you married?
Nigel Depends on how you want to look at it, love. He's not there then, is he? My dad?
Nurse He wasn't ten minutes ago. Your mother is though and has been for quarter of an hour. (*She takes out the thermometer, checks it and returns it to its holder on the wall*) Well, at least that's back to normal.
Nigel (*over-acting*) My God! I'm normal! What am I going to do? I'll never work again!

The Nurse laughs as she enters the details on to Nigel's chart

Ruby's face appears in the window the other side of the room door. She stretches here and there but can't see very much

Nurse Behave yourself. Oh, by the way; what religion are you?
Nigel Church of England, love. What else would a queen be?
Nurse Are you gay, Nigel?
Nigel Is the Pope Catholic?
Nurse Are you a practising homosexual?
Nigel No, love, I'm perfect at it.
Nurse Be serious. I hope you take precautions.

Nigel puts his hand on his chest as if to enquire what the Nurse means

Condoms.
Nigel Oh, God, no, love. I can't get on with them. I use cling-film. I roll my own.
Nurse (*to Vernon, laughing*) How do you put up with him?

Vernon doesn't answer but he tries to smile

Nigel Have you finished with my body?
Nurse Not quite. I'm going to get you a clean dressing for your head. (*She turns to go*)

Ruby sees the Nurse walking towards her and quickly disappears

Nigel Have you got time to do my nails as well?
Nurse (*laughing again*) This is a hospital not a beauty salon.
Nigel Never! I *thought* I was in the wrong place!
Nurse (*laughing*) You're mad.
Nigel Did I tell you about the fat man and the girl with the wooden eye?
Nurse I'll be back in a minute.

The Nurse exits

Ruby (*off*) Is that it, nurse? Can I go in now?
Nigel It's a hell of a waste, isn't it?
Vernon What?
Nigel (*giving his nails a quick look over*) The way I have with women. Kev isn't half as good at it.
Vernon Does that surprise you?
Nigel Well, yes, it does, yes — under the circumstances.
Vernon How do you mean?
Nigel Well, he doesn't look much like you. I would have thought he'd have inherited at least one of your — what would you call them — virtues? (*He smiles and stares at Vernon*)

Vernon stares back at Nigel for a moment, then looks away

Where is he anyway? He hasn't come in to see me yet.
Vernon Why did you introduce me as your father-in-law?
Nigel Because that's how I see you. Anyway, you told me to call you it once.
Vernon (*turning to him*) When?
Nigel One night when you were pissed out of your brain.
Vernon You mean the night we had a couple of lagers together?
Griff (*off, shouting*) I meant it then, and accident or no I mean it now.
Nigel The old man's here then. God, now the shit will hit the fan.
Ruby (*off, raising her voice*) Don't talk like that. He might never come out of there.
Nigel Listen to her. She's dramatic beyond.

During the following Vernon turns away to look out of the door

Griff (*off, shouting*) He's got a couple of bruises, a few cracked ribs and a knock on the head. He's not going to die, Ruby. He'll be out of this place by Thursday — you take it from me.
Nigel I hope he's right — I got a dress fitting Friday, eleven o'clock. (*He gives a small laugh, then realizes that Vernon is turned away from him. A slight pause*) I'm sorry, I embarrassed you in front of the nurse, didn't I?
Vernon I just feel there's a time and place for everything.
Nigel Yes, you're right ... and I'm sorry. I don't know what's the matter with me. I just can't seem to stop myself going one step over the mark. I do it all the time. I did it on Saturday. I wasn't happy to get my old man up on stage and give him a good time, if you know what I mean. No. I had to go and reveal myself to him, didn't I, in front of all those people.
Vernon It must have been awful for him.
Nigel It wasn't wonderful for me, love.
Vernon (*turning towards Nigel*) Then why did you do it?

Nigel I don't know. I never know. There I am living my life with everything going all right, and then all of a sudden for no reason at all I say or do something that's completely over the top. I just get carried away and I don't know why. It's frightening, isn't it?

Vernon Perhaps you should learn to exercise a bit more control.

Nigel (*agreeing whole-heartedly*) Yes — doesn't sound half as much fun though, does it? (*He laughs*) Where the hell has Kevin got to, do you think? I want him to bring a weekend case in. I can't see them keeping me in much longer, can you?

Vernon You've had an accident, Nigel. The car's a write-off, have they told you?

Nigel They haven't told me anything, love. It's like the frigging secret service in this place. You come in with concussion and they treat you like you've got three months to live. They're keeping something from me, though, I know they are.

Vernon You were quite poorly yesterday.

Nigel Yes, but today I've made a brilliant recovery. All right, I'm bruised all over, but it only hurts when I laugh. Bed rest, that's all I need, and I can have that in the house.

Vernon I think you're here for a couple of days yet.

Nigel How do you know? Have they said something?

Vernon They're hardly going to say anything to *me*.

Nigel That's what I mean. It's easier to get information out of the DHSS.

Vernon I think you'd do best to rest up and not worry about anything.

Nigel I suppose you're right. (*A slight pause*) How come you're here?

Vernon What?

Nigel And so early. Even before the old girl and that's saying something.

Vernon doesn't answer, just shakes his head

A pause

Vernon (*crossing to chair R of the bed*) What happened? Do you remember?

Nigel With the car?

Vernon nods

We weren't drunk or anything ... neither of us. We don't drink when we're working, though I felt like it on Saturday.

Vernon You veered off the road for no apparent reason. The car's wrecked and you've made one hell of a mess of a thirty-foot oak.

Nigel You've seen it then?

Vernon The car?

Nigel The tree. You've been there. Seen the damage.
Vernon Er ... no. (*He walks to the* L *around the bed*)

Nigel waits for an explanation

That policeman said. Earlier on. (*A slight pause*) You don't remember?

Nigel shakes his head

Maybe that knock on the head has done more damage than you think.
Nigel I remember everything, but don't remember him saying anything about a thirty-foot oak.
Vernon Perhaps it was a birch, then. (*He shrugs it off. A slight pause*) When you say you remember everything ...
Nigel I mean, I remember everything.

They look at each other. A pause

Vernon You told the policeman you fell asleep at the wheel.
Nigel I'd have told him anything to get rid of him. Ohh, he had terrible bad breath, did you notice? If he hasn't got halitosis, love, I'm not one of the Dolly Sisters.
Vernon That's not what happened then? You didn't fall asleep at the wheel?
Nigel It was good enough for him.
Vernon Meaning it's good enough for me?
Nigel I didn't say that.
Vernon Tell me what happened.
Nigel What do you want to know?
Vernon The truth.
Nigel (*after a slight pause*) I'll make a deal with you. I'll be honest with you if you'll be honest with me.

There is a pause; Vernon comes to sit at the bottom of the bed facing the audience

Vernon You saw me, didn't you?
Nigel When?
Vernon Saturday night. At the pull-in. Half-way through Coedcae Lane — the picnic area. (*He stands and rambles on*) It didn't mean anything, and I've never done it before. I don't want to hurt Rita. It was just one of those things, you know, a one-off ...

Nigel appears to be hearing all of this for the first time

(*Turning to look at Nigel and realizing he's put his foot in it*) You didn't see me, did you?

Nigel No.

Vernon Shit!

Nigel But you saw me obviously.

Vernon (*moving around the bed to* C) I was convinced you ——

Nigel I saw a car parked there but I didn't recognize it.

Vernon I thought you'd followed me. I thought Kevin had smelled a rat and you'd followed me.

Nigel We were coming back from our gig, Vern. I stopped for a pee, that's all.

A pause

Vernon What happens now?

Nigel Meaning am I going to tell Kevin?

Vernon Meaning are you going to tell his mother?

Nigel I wouldn't do that.

Vernon Good, that's a weight off my mind.

Nigel Well, not to Rita anyway. Kevin, now — that's a different story.

Vernon Can't you keep it to yourself? I mean it's not as if it's going to happen again.

Nigel We don't have any secrets between us. We're painfully honest with each other. Ask him if you don't believe me.

Vernon Perhaps you won't tell Rita but Kevin might. (*He turns to look at Nigel*) It's not all that long ago we — well, you know ...

Nigel What?

Vernon We're really close now. I don't want anything to upset it all.

Nigel No doubt that slipped your mind when you pulled into Coedcae Lane, popped into the back seat with whoever she was and got down to it. You surprise me, Vernon, I didn't think you were one to put it around.

Vernon I'm not! I've told you — it's never happened before. (*He looks out of the window*)

Nigel You only ever did it once and you got caught. Christ, Vern, you really were shit out of luck.

Vernon Suddenly it was on a plate and I took it.

Nigel Aaaah, an opportunist shagger.

Vernon Rita ... well, the last eighteen months she hasn't been ... know what I mean? She hasn't been interested in me at all. Not in that way.

Nigel You'll have me feeling sorry for you in a minute.

Vernon It's not natural for a man to go that long.

Nigel It's not natural for a man of your age to be in that position in the back of a car in Coedcae Lane.

Vernon So you did see me then?

Nigel I saw a load of arms and legs. I tried to get a better look and peed over my foot. Ruined a fabulous pair of shoes.

Vernon Can I trust you not to say anything?

Nigel (*after a slight pause*) That's why you're here, isn't it? You thought I saw you and you wanted to gag me. And there's me thinking you were in here because you were worried about me; well thank you very much, Vern.

Vernon I am worried about you — I'm just worried about Rita finding out as well. She mustn't, Nigel. (*A slight pause*) We've been married twenty-five years next month.

Nigel Happy anniversary.

Vernon She's planning a big do.

Nigel I know, I'm the cabaret.

Vernon If Rita found out she'd kill me.

Nigel Have you made a will then, Vern? I should if I were you.

Vernon Don't joke about it.

Nigel Who's joking?

Vernon You're going to give me away, then?

Nigel doesn't answer

One mistake and ffittt. Gone. I lose everything.

Nigel You're not going to lose nothing. I reckon we're all allowed to make one mistake, don't you? Look at me on Saturday.

Ruby (*off, shouting*) So you'd have rather he had died up there on that stage then, would you?

Griff (*off, shouting*) Yes.

Ruby (*off, shouting*) Is that what you're saying?

Griff (*off, shouting*) Yes!

Nigel Poor sod.

Vernon It's not easy for him. I know, I've been there.

Nigel He's pathetic.

Vernon He's your father.

Nigel That only makes it worse. (*A slight pause*) I said I didn't know why I did it but the truth is I did. (*A slight pause*) I looked down at him from the stage and there he was gripping his pint, looking so butch and laughing from arsehole to breakfast. (*A slight pause*) God knows why but suddenly I remembered the time when he came home from work and saw me knitting. He went apeshit — and now here he is I thought having the laugh of his life and I was giving it to him. It was cruel, I know, but he had it coming — for years he had it coming. I'm sorry now of course.

Vernon That's something at least. (*He sits in the chair next to the bed*)

Nigel Not that I'd tell him. He doesn't deserve it so don't you say anything either. (*A slight pause*) You and I are not all that different when you stop and think about it, are we?

Vernon How do you work that out?

Nigel We didn't mind putting our hands in the fire at the time — but today? Today we don't want to have our fingers burnt.

Vernon Hang on, I thought you weren't going to say anything.

Nigel I'm not. Your secret is safe with me, don't worry.

Vernon What will you tell Kevin?

Nigel Nothing. What he doesn't know won't harm him, I suppose.

Vernon nods and smiles; there is a slight pause

Vernon You still haven't told me what happened on Saturday. (*He gets up and moves down* R) All I know is that you weren't drunk and you didn't fall asleep at the wheel.

Nigel What has Kevin told you?

Vernon (*after a slight pause*) Nothing yet.

Nigel And he won't. Not until he's spoken to me first. Where did you say he was? He is here you said, isn't he?

Vernon He's just down the corridor.

Nigel Fetch him for me then, Vern, please? Tell him I'm waiting to see him.

Vernon He was in the car too, you know.

Nigel I know that. Look, I might have had a knock on the head but I haven't forgotten who was with ... (*He suddenly realizes the implication of what Vernon has said*) What are you trying to say? What's going on? Is he a patient here? Is he hurt?

Vernon You got off lucky.

Nigel He is, isn't he? What's happened? Is he all right? (*He raises his voice*) Tell me what's going on!

Vernon (*shouting back*) You should never have been in those lanes.

Nigel That's great coming from you! What's the situation?

Vernon (*after a slight pause*) He's got some head injuries.

Nigel (*after a slight pause*) Oh, that's all right then. (*A slight pause*) It is all right, isn't it? Is it an injury like mine or what?

Vernon We'll know more later.

Nigel I want to see him. (*He struggles to help himself out of bed*)

Vernon What are you doing?

Nigel What's his room number?

Vernon You can't go to him.

Nigel Try and stop me.

Vernon There's only one allowed in at a time.

Nigel So?
Vernon Rita's in there.
Nigel (*after a slight pause*) It's serious, isn't it? It must be for you both to be here.
Vernon Both your parents are here and you might be home by the weekend.
Nigel So it's not serious. Is that what you're saying?

Vernon doesn't answer

(*Shouting*) What are you saying! Tell me what's going on!
Griff (*off, shouting*) No, I said! You bloody deaf or what?

There is a slight pause

The Nurse enters the room carrying a tray with bandages, scissors and plaster, et cetera. She stops just inside the room and looks from Nigel to Vernon. She senses something is wrong

Nurse What's up? (*To Nigel*) And no wisecracks.
Nigel I want to know what you're keeping from me.
Nurse What makes you think we're keeping anything.
Nigel I'm not stupid. I know something's going on.
Nurse Oh, that. (*She indicates that she means Griff shouting in the corridor*) Your father's arrived but he's not staying. He's going on to work. I asked him if he ——
Nigel I'm not on about him. I don't give a shit about him.
Nurse (*moving to the bed and preparing to renew Nigel's head dressing*) Well, that's not very nice.
Nigel (*raising his voice*) What's happened to Kevin?
Nurse Kevin who?
Nigel If somebody doesn't start giving me some answers, I'm going to scream!
Nurse Now this isn't going to hurt. (*She starts to take the old dressing from Nigel's forehead*)

All of a sudden Nigel screams

I've hardly touched you.

Nigel clenches his fists and makes the most frustrating noise possible

Vernon Tell him, go on. (*A slight pause*) Kevin Edwards. Room four. Tell him.

There is a slight pause. During the following, the Nurse continues to change the dressing

Nurse Well — it's early days yet. We'll know more in the next forty-eight hours. We've had patients like him in before and they've made a complete recovery so I wouldn't get too alarmed at this stage.

Nigel I don't believe you! (*He raises his voice*) You should be a politician not a nurse. You just made me a speech and told me sod all!

Nurse (*raising her voice*) Keep still.

Vernon (*shouting*) He's unconscious! (*A slight pause; quieter now*) He hasn't come round since the accident.

Nothing is said for a while. After a time the Nurse removes Nigel's dirty dressing with metal tweezers

Nurse There you are, how's that? (*She disposes of the dressing in a paper bag and continues to re-dress the wound*)

Nigel I want to see him.

Nurse You've got no chance, sunshine. You can't get out of bed.

Nigel If I could, would you take me?

Nurse No.

Nigel Why?

Nurse It's family only.

Nigel You've got to be joking. (*To Vernon*) Did you hear what she said? (*To the Nurse*) I am family. (*To Vernon*) Tell her who I am.

Vernon doesn't answer

(*Shouting at Vernon*) Tell her!

Nurse I have grasped the situation.

Nigel And?

Nurse Rules are rules.

Nigel I've got to see him, don't you understand? And he'd want to see me anyway.

Vernon Would he?

Nigel Of course he would. Come on, Vern, how can you say that?

Vernon I'm still in the dark. Something's up. If I knew what really happened on Saturday ...

Nigel (*to the Nurse*) Please. Fix it for me?

Nurse Andrea my name is, not Jimmy Savile.

Nigel I'll do all the jokes if you don't mind. What do you say? Can you sort it out for me?

Nurse I'd have to get permission.

Nigel From who, the staff?
Nurse And the family.
Nigel Well, that part's easy. Vern, tell her it's OK

Vernon doesn't answer

Vernon?
Vernon It's not me ... it's Rita.
Nigel What?
Vernon She's upset ... and she doesn't want ...
Nigel What?
Vernon (*after a slight pause*) She doesn't want anyone to see him.
Nigel Even me?
Vernon Especially you.
Nigel Why?
Vernon Work it out for yourself.
Nigel (*after a slight pause*) I want to see him, Vern, so you'd better fix it.
Vernon I don't think I can.
Nigel Try.
Vernon She's very upset.
Nigel She's not half as upset as she'd be if I had a word with her. Do you
   follow me? Do you understand what I'm saying here, Vern?
Vernon Give her a day or two — she'll calm down.
Nurse I'd give her longer than that. (*She opens a clean dressing*)
Nigel I want to see him now.
Vernon Why rock the boat?
Nigel Rock it? I'll sink it if I have to.
Nurse I think you'd better try and get yourself better before you start to worry
   about anyone else.
Nigel Oh, piss off!
Nurse (*outraged*) I beg your pardon!
Nigel Look, are you married? Of course you are, you've got a little girl.
Nurse I'm divorced. Why?
Nigel Nothing. It doesn't matter. Don't you understand? Don't either of you
   understand?
Vernon There's nothing you can do for him. The nurse is right. (*He sits in
   the chair next to the bed*) Get yourself well first, then worry about Kevin.
Nigel I want to see Rita then.
Vernon What?
Nigel What's the matter, Vern? (*To the Nurse*) The colour's drained right out
   of his face, look.

The Nurse puts a clean dressing on Nigel's forehead

Vernon (*getting up and moving down* R) The way things are at the moment, the further I keep you two apart the better.
Nigel Would that be for my sake or yours?

Vernon doesn't answer

I just want to talk to her that's all. Nothing to do with you and Saturday night. You don't honestly think I'm going to tell her that I saw your lily white bum bobbing up and down in the moonlight? (*To the Nurse*) I did.

Vernon buries his head in his hands

She blames me, doesn't she?
Vernon She always said you drove too fast. (*To the Nurse*) There's no truth in what he said nurse, he just did it to embarrass me.
Nigel It wasn't my fault — not really.
Vernon You saying it's Kevin's fault then?
Nigel We were ... there was ...
Nurse You were having a domestic, that's what happened, wasn't it?

There is a slight pause

Vernon Was it?
Nigel (*to the Nurse*) How did you know?
Nurse Been there, darling, and done it. (*A slight pause*) I'm divorced, aren't I? I recognize the signs. It doesn't take a genius.
Vernon Is that what happened? You and Kevin had a row?
Nigel (*after a slight pause*) Yeah. That's about the long and short of it, yeah.
Vernon Serious?
Nigel We crashed the fucking car, didn't we? (*A pause*) I've been saying for weeks that there's something up but he kept denying it. Why he chose to tell me there and then in the car God only knows.
Vernon Tell you what?
Nurse They're splitting up.
Nigel Do you mind! (*A slight pause*) He's chucking it all in, Vern. Me, him, the act, the lot. I kept screaming at him to think about what he was giving up, but you know Kevin, when he's got something in his head ... Four years together and a promising career all down the Swanee.
Vernon (*after a slight pause*) I'm sure he didn't mean it. People say a lot of things when they're arguing.
Nigel (*shouting*) That's why we were arguing, you silly bloody ... (*He pulls himself together*) All right, I said, you think we're all washed up — but you can't go back.
Nurse Back?

Vernon Back?

Nigel Yes. It's a big mistake to think you can go back, I said.

Vernon To where?

Nigel To who.

Vernon To who then?

Nigel To who do you think? His cowing wife, that's who.

Nurse You're kidding.

Vernon Are you sure?

Nigel No, I'm making it up because I enjoy being this hysterical. (*A slight pause*) He's been seeing her for the past couple of weeks.

Nurse I'd better carry on.(*During the following, she fills in Nigel's chart at the bottom of the bed*)

Nigel Yes, why not, every bugger else is.

Griff (*off; shouting*) Will you tell me what the hell's happening to us?

Ruby (*off; shouting*) Will you keep your voice down? You're in a hospital, remember.

Griff (*off; shouting*) I don't care where I am. Up till last Saturday our family was quite — orthodox.

Nigel Orthodox?

Ruby (*off; shouting*) Orthodox? Good God, Griff, you can call us a lot of things but we've hardly been that.

Griff (*off; shouting*) On the surface we were. Now all of a sudden everything's a mess.

Nigel You can say that again.

Griff (*off; shouting*) A mess!

Nigel (*to the Nurse*) I thought he'd have gone home by now.

Vernon When is all this supposed to be happening with you and Kevin?

Nigel (*after a slight pause*) "You're making a big mistake," I said. "You can't change your whole lifestyle just like that"— but he was having none of it. "What about me?" I said. "What's going to happen to me? I love you. Where do I stand in all this?" Next week apparently, Vernon. He's moving out next week. I knew we had problems but I didn't think it was anything on that scale.

Nurse My fella went and I didn't even know he'd gone till I had a phone call.

Nigel So I'm supposed to be grateful now, am I?

Nurse Didn't even say "So long" to his daughter.

Nigel I'm not going to be able to say *"Hallo"* to mine.

Vernon (*firmly*) Kate isn't your daughter, Nigel.

Nigel She was going to be. When there was a problem and that cow of a mother didn't want her, what did I say? I said, "It's all right, Kev. We'll have her come to us." How many others would have said that? I was going to give up my day job to look after her. It was all planned. I mean we've told people.

Vernon (*moving towards the bed*) Kate was going to live with you?

Nigel You'd have seen more of her then, I could have promised you that.
Vernon You and Kevin couldn't have brought Kate up, Nigel.
Nigel Why not?
Vernon It wouldn't have been right. She needs a mother and a father. All kids do.
Nigel Oh, wake up, Vern. Even I'd have made a damned sight better mother than the one that doesn't love her now.
Vernon Why has he made the decision to go back? I can't work it out.
Nurse (*to Vernon*) He probably told him why in the car. That's what the row was about.
Nigel I thought we were happy. I think I could have accepted it more if it was another man ... but his wife.
Vernon It doesn't make sense. I can't understand why he would run back to her?
Nurse He's not running *to* her, he's running *from* him.

Nigel looks rather incredulously at the Nurse

Well, that's how I see it anyway.
Nigel No, you're wrong. He's running from *himself.* "I want to be normal," he said. Christ — don't we all?
Vernon Wait till Rita finds out.
Nigel It'll be just up her street.
Vernon You've got to be joking. You might not be her favourite person at the moment, but she likes you. She's hated Erica from day one.
Griff (*off, shouting*) There was nothing funny about me and Ritchie. We were like brothers, we were.
Ruby (*off, shouting*) You don't take your brother on honeymoon with you.
Griff (*off, shouting*) I didn't take him on honeymoon.
Ruby (*off, shouting*) It's a hell of a coincidence that he ended up in the caravan next to us then, don't you think?
Nurse (*to Nigel*) And you thought *you* had trouble.
Vernon He took a mate on honeymoon? What sort of family are you?
Nigel I don't think you're in a position to criticize, do you? (*A slight pause*) I didn't know about that though ... (*He indicates that he means his father and his friend*) And who the hell is Ritchie, anyway?
Nurse There you are. Let me help you up.

The Nurse helps Nigel sit up

All right? Ready for your visitors then?
Nigel I wish they'd all go home. (*To Vernon*) You included.
Nurse You don't mean that. I'll send them in, shall I?

Nigel Why not. It's like a cowing three-ringed circus in here anyway.
Nurse I can send them all away if that's what you want. You don't have to
see anyone.

Nigel doesn't reply

Nigel?
Nigel Do what you like.

The Nurse covers a smile. She makes to turn away with her tray of things

Vernon (*stopping the Nurse*) You didn't believe him, did you, nurse?

The Nurse doesn't understand

You know ... the bum ... the moonlight. It's a load of rubbish.

*The Nurse takes a breath, not really knowing how to react. She shakes her
head and her eyes widen. She exhales through her nose and smiles, turns
and exits*

A pause

I think I pulled that off. (*A pause*) Perhaps I'd better go too, then.
Nigel Yes, go on, go. Talk about rats and the sinking ship.
Vernon You wanted me to leave a minute ago.
Nigel You've had what you came for so you can bugger off now if you want
to.
Vernon That's not fair. I'll stay as long as you want me to. (*Pause*) Of course
I was hoping to have a word with you about ... well, you know ... but I do
care about you. We both do, Rita and myself.

A slight pause

Nigel When we met — I mean when *we* met — (*he indicates himself and
Vernon*) when Kevin brought me to your house, you were both marvellous
about it. I wasn't sure if you were on my side, but at least you weren't
against me ...
Vernon Yes ...
Nigel I'm just wondering where you stand now. Do you approve of his plans
or not?
Vernon Do you want the truth?
Nigel And nothing but.

Vernon I don't know. Up until a quarter of an hour ago I didn't know anything about them.

Nigel You must have had a gut reaction when I told you. What are you feeling, Vern? I can't work it out.

Vernon (*shaking his head and thinking about it*) I want what he wants I suppose.

Nigel What if he doesn't know what he wants? What if he turned to you tomorrow and said, "Dad, talk to me. I'm all mixed up and I need help". What would you say then, Vern?

A pause

Vernon (*moving to the bed*) You are one of the better things that happened to Kevin.

Nigel Remind him then, will you, because he's forgotten.

Vernon Well, we haven't. Whatever happens between you, me and Rita will always be grateful for what you did for him.

Nigel I can't take all the credit. You made it easy for me.

Vernon We just wanted what was best for him — at the time there was no doubt about it.

Nigel At the time? What about now? What about now, Vern?

Vernon I don't know. I thought you were happy too.

Nigel Hey, listen, I didn't influence him.

Vernon Of course not.

Nigel He was well aware of his preferences before he met me.

Vernon I know that. (*A slight pause. He sits on the L side of the bed*) We knew how things were with him long before you came along ... or at least we thought we knew. Although he never talked about his ... preferences, as you say, me and Rita, we assumed. (*A slight pause*) Then one day he surprised us and brought Erica home. Surprised? We were gob-smacked. I was delighted, I encouraged it even though Rita didn't like her. I was so glad to be wrong about him. I kept telling Rita he'd grow out of it and now I thought he'd proved me right. I pushed him into that marriage and it all but destroyed him.

Nigel So what are you saying? You saying he should stay with me or what?

Vernon When he left his wife, Rita thought he might have come home to us. We waited but there was no word, nothing. London was the last place we thought he'd have run to. That was the worst year of our lives. Then one day the phone rang ——

Nigel I know — I dialled it.

Vernon We couldn't believe it when he got in touch. We didn't mind even when he wrote and said you were in tow.

Nigel Oh, that's very kind of you.

Vernon No offence meant. (*He stands*)

Nigel Well, plenty taken.

Vernon Anything he wanted to do was all right by us at the time, we were so glad to have him back. I felt guilty ——

Nigel And responsible for the mess he'd made of his marriage, yeah, Vern, I've heard of all this before.

Vernon You know how long it took him to forgive me and to pick up the pieces. I don't want to say anything that might put us back to square one.

Nigel There you are, you see? I knew if I pushed you hard enough I'd get you to show your hand.

Vernon No, you don't understand.

Nigel But I do, Vern. I understand perfectly. Kevin can do whatever he likes. He can toss me aside like stinking lettuce if he wants to because the bottom line here is that whatever he wants is all right with you.

Vernon Look. (*A slight pause*) When you lose someone — well, it's awful.

Nigel Tell me about it!

Vernon If you're lucky enough to get them back — you put up with a lot just to hang on to them.

Nigel I'll bear that in mind.

Vernon I know you're hurting. And you're probably upset because you think I've let you down ...

Nigel Good God no, Vern, what makes you think that! (*A slight pause*) You're unbelievable. (*A slight pause*) Do you know what I think? Vern? Everything's falling into place now. I think it was all an act with you. Oh, not this here now today, I meant you and me from day one. You remember that day, Vern? It was the day Kevin introduced me and you put your arm on my shoulder and said "Welcome to the family" — but you didn't approve of me at all. It was all an act, wasn't it? I was "put up" with for Kevin's sake. I was all right just as long as I was what he wanted, but the minute you think he wants something else, you see your chance and you dump on me — and you've dumped on me from a great height.

Vernon I understand how you feel.

Nigel Do you?

Vernon Of course.

Nigel Tell me then. (*A slight pause; raising his voice*). Go on, tell me how I feel.

Vernon doesn't answer

(*Quieter*) You haven't a clue. You couldn't even comprehend it. I feel less than nothing. Less than that piece of dandruff on your shoulder there. Even a piece of dandruff is a piece of dandruff. Me? I'm just a freak; it doesn't matter that I'm a very good freak, that I'm a talented freak. In your eyes and the eyes of my old man out there, I'm just a piece of shit. The only difference between you is that you want to flush me away, and him? I'm the accident in his pants — he can't get rid of me that easily. He thinks I'm the big embarrassment people won't let him forget but the truth is — the truth is he won't let himself forget. (*A slight pause*) No, Vern, believe me, you couldn't possibly know how I feel.

Ruby (*off*) Roots and wings, Griff — remember roots and wings.

Nigel Fathers — they make me sick. (*A slight pause*) I'd make a better parent than either of you put together.

Vernon (*after a pause*) If there's anything I can do.

Nigel Don't make me laugh. You know I wish people wouldn't say that, they rarely mean it.

Vernon Will you be all right?

Nigel Oh, don't worry about me yet, Vern. There's a lot more talking to be done yet.

Vernon But you said it was over.

Nigel No, not quite. It's not over till the fat lady sings.

Vernon What?

Nigel shakes his head and gestures for Vernon to forget it

Nigel How can you do it to him?

Vernon What?

Nigel You said yourself that living with a woman all but destroyed him.

Vernon I'm just going to be there for him, that's all.

Nigel You're walking on very thin ice, Vern. Be warned, when it's that thin you're bound to get yourself wet.

Vernon I'm not going to make the same mistake twice if that's what you're worried about.

Nigel You bet your arse you're not, because if I've got anything to do with it you're not going to have the opportunity.

Vernon What do you mean?

Nigel I've put too much into this relationship to throw it away.

Vernon What are you going to do?

Nigel The only thing I know how. I'm going to fight! I love him too much to give him up without a scrap. I'll take on you, him, Rita and that tart of a wife if I have to.

Vernon (*almost afraid to ask*) What have you got in mind? You're not going to start throwing mud, are you?

Nigel Mud? I'm going to throw everything I can get my hands on, love.

Vernon (*very worried*) When you say everything ...

Nigel I mean — everything! I wouldn't be at all surprised if Rita doesn't end up cancelling that silver wedding do.

Vernon You wouldn't.

Nigel All's fair in love and war, Vern. I'd get very worried and start panicking if I were you.

Ruby enters

Ruby There you are! Oooh, you're much better today. How are you feeling, all right?

Nigel A hundred per cent. One hundred per cent. Sit down, Ma, 'cos it's ... showtime!

The introduction to Shirley Bassey's "I Am What I Am" begins

Ruby stands and looks agog. She does not see Vernon standing a yard or two behind her

The Lights snap off leaving the stage in darkness

Just as Bassey begins to sing ——

—— the CURTAIN *falls*

ACT II

*The stage is divided in two, with half the room and half the corridor visible;
one of the double doors is now red, representing the door inside the room,
and the other blue to represent the corridor outside*

*The music played at the end of Act I starts at exactly the same place. After
Shirley Bassey has sung the first line, the sound cross-fades from this to her
singing the last two lines or so of the final verse. As this cross-fade takes place,
the Lights come up*

*The action is continuous. Ruby and Vernon are holding the same positions
as when we last saw them. Nigel is singing along with Shirley Bassey, his
hands held up in the air*

The singing and music finish. There is a slight pause

Ruby What the hell was all that about?
Nigel Mam, this is Vernon.
Ruby What? (*She turns round and sees Vernon for the first time*) Oooh. (*She
laughs nervously in an attempt to save her embarrassment*) Hallo Doctor.
I'm Nigel's mother.
Nigel He's not the doctor.
Ruby You'll have to excuse my son. (*Almost mouthing the words*) He's in
show business. (*She suddenly realizes what Nigel has just said and turns
to him*) What?
Nigel This is Kevin's father.
Ruby (*looking immediately at Vernon; after a slight pause*) Of course you
are. You're a spit of him, has anyone ever told you? (*A thought strikes her*)
Wait a minute. (*She moves to the other side of the bed, standing to the L of
Nigel*) What's he doing in here before me?
Nigel Would you like to answer that one, Vern?

Griff sheepishly opens the door to the room and steps inside

Ruby (*pleased with herself*) Oh, look, Nigel — your father's come in to see
you.

Nigel (*singing the theme song from the TV show*) "Mr and Mrs, da da da da da da, love one another."

Griff What's going on?

Nigel (*launching into a mock game-show*) Right, here we go then folks. Ready for your first three questions? This is for your mother, OK? If you caught my father having sex in the back of a car, would you (a) change your address, (b) change your car, or (c) change your husband?

Ruby (*to Vernon*) How long has he been like this?

Vernon Ever since I've known him.

Nigel Wrong. (*He makes a noise like a buzzer*) Next. Your turn, Vern. If you took a mate with you on honeymoon, what would your wife say? Would she say, (a) I don't care how close you are he's not putting his boots under my bed, (b) is that bed going to be big enough for all of us, or, (c) we can't all sleep together, I wouldn't know which way to turn?

Griff (*to Ruby*) Did you hear that? That's all your fault, that is.

Ruby Mine?

Nigel Wrong! (*He makes another buzzing noise*) You're next, Griff. If your only son turned out to be gay, would you (a) find him a girlfriend, (b) find him a boyfriend, or (c) find him a shrink to straighten him out?

Ruby (*shouting to Griff*) I told you to keep your voice down.

Griff (*shouting*) I don't shout!

Ruby You're shouting now. And look at your colour. (*To Vernon, smiling*) Least little thing and he's red as a beetroot. He can't help it, he suffers with hypertension.

Griff I don't know why I bothered coming in here.

Ruby Of course you do.

Griff (*shouting*) And there's nothing wrong with my blood pressure!

Ruby You know there is. One day you'll start telling yourself the truth.

Nigel Seems to me we all live in "Secret City", don't you agree, Vern? Dad?

Rita comes in from L. She is a woman in her early forties. She looks wrecked as she's been at the hospital for just over twenty-four hours. She is extremely uptight and is very anxious about the condition of her son; she also has a few other things on her mind. She makes for the coffee machine and looks for change in her purse

Griff I should never have listened to you. So much for that smile you said I'd get.

Ruby Nigel, smile for your father.

Vernon I'd better go.

Nigel (*to Vernon*) Don't even think about it.

Ruby Nigel.

The Nurse enters the hallway from R

Nurse (*seeing Rita*) Oh ... hiya.
Vernon You don't want me here, it's a family thing.
Nurse All right?
Nigel You are family — for a bit longer, anyway.
Nurse How's Kevin doing?
Griff I'd better go.
Rita (*searching her purse*) The same.
Ruby (*to Griff*) You just dare, Nigel!
Nigel What?
Ruby (*after a slight pause*) I've forgotten what I wanted you for now.
Nurse No change?
Rita Yes — I just need a bigger purse I suppose.
Ruby (*remembering*) Oh, I know. Haven't you got anything to say to your
    father?
Nurse You sure you're all right?

Rita nods. She's not really all right

Nigel Yeah, good night Saturday, wasn't it?
Griff Right, that's it. (*He makes to go*)
Nurse See you then.
Ruby Griff!
Griff You heard that, didn't you?

The Nurse exits looking slightly concerned about Rita

During the following, Rita gets a cup of coffee from the machine

Vernon I'm not very comfortable here.
Nigel So, squirm.
Ruby Nigel!
Rita (*calling after her*) Nurse!
Ruby There was no need to say that to your father.
Griff I should never have come in here.

The Nurse appears in the corridor

Griff I don't know why I let you talk me into it.
Nurse (*to Rita*) Yes?
Ruby Nigel, do your mother a favour and give your father a smile.

*Nigel gives Griff a very quick, false smile putting both thumbs under his chin
as he cocks his head to one side*

Griff (*infuriatedly*) It's like a mad house here ...
Rita (*shaking her head*) Nothing ... it's all right.

The Nurse leaves

Griff (*turning to go*) I'm going to work.
Ruby Griff?
Griff (*with his back to Ruby*) You can say what you like — me and him are finished. (*He heads for the door*)
Nigel Did we ever start?
Ruby No, don't say that. (*To Griff*) He didn't mean what he said. He's all mixed up — he's probably delirious.

Griff exits through the blue door and immediately enters through the red door which leads him into the corridor. He literally bumps into Rita who has a cup of coffee in her hand; some coffee spills on to the floor

Ruby (*to Nigel*) Well ... you've done it now.
Nigel No, I haven't done it *now*. I did it last Saturday.
Griff Oh, I'm sorry.
Nigel And I'm not sorry.
Ruby (*getting upset*) I can't take much more of this. I've had a gutsful between the pair of you.
Vernon (*to Ruby*) Are you all right?
Rita (*to Griff, very impatiently*) I'm fine, I'm fine.

Griff and Vernon get out their handkerchiefs to offer them to Rita and Ruby respectively

Griff Here.
Vernon Have a hanky.
Ruby It's all right, I've got one. (*She takes one out of her pocket*)

Rita takes Griff's hanky and begins to use it to dry herself

Griff Sit down, come on.
Ruby (*snappily*) No, I'm all right.
Vernon Tea?
Rita No.
Griff Are you sure?
Ruby Yes.
Vernon Coffee?
Rita All right.

Griff I'll bring it over.

Rita sits down. Griff gets two cups of coffee from the machine during the following

Ruby dries her nose. As she is doing so, Vernon mouths to Nigel to "Let me go". Nigel smiles and shakes his head. Ruby sees this however and is suspicious

Ruby There's nothing going on here, is there?
Vernon Like what?
Ruby I don't know.
Nigel She's very quick, my mother.
Ruby So I'm right then, am I?
Vernon (*quickly*) No.
Nigel You answered that a bit too sharply then, Vern. You'll never convince her now.
Ruby You are who you say you are, are you?
Vernon What do you mean?
Nigel She's inferring you might be some sort of extra-marital affair. Am I right, Mother?
Ruby Well ...
Vernon You're barking up the wrong tree there.
Nigel Good God, yes. Vernon loves women, don't you, Vern? Oh, and by the way, I don't want either of you to mention trees for the rest of the day, is that understood?
Ruby Trees?
Vernon It's what they collided into.

Griff goes over to Rita and hands her a coffee before sitting down next to her

Rita Thanks.
Griff You're still a bit wet.
Rita It's nothing — really.

A pause

Ruby You've gone and let me down as far as your father's concerned, you know that, don't you?
Nigel I've been letting you down as far as he's concerned ever since I was born.
Ruby Now there's no need for that. (*To Vernon*) Griff thinks the world of him really. (*To Nigel*) And you love him too if the truth be known.

Rita is more than a little shaky and upset. She runs her hand through her hair in an attempt to pull herself together

Griff Trouble?
Rita Sorry?
Griff You look a bit ... you know.
Rita It's been a long night.
Griff It's been a long weekend.
Ruby (*to Vernon*) You know, I've been rabbiting on here, you must think I'm very rude. I haven't asked you once how Kevin's doing.
Vernon He's holding his own.
Nigel Well it's a change from holding mine. (*He laughs*)

No-one joins him

I'm sorry. That wasn't funny, was it?
Ruby That's the trouble with you. You never know how far to go.
Griff Who is it? Father? Husband?
Ruby If you knew what it took to get your father to come in here.
Rita Son.
Griff Snap.
Nigel It shouldn't have taken anything.
Ruby It wasn't easy for him. He was offering you an olive branch.
Nigel (*yawning*) Now you know what I said about trees! Oh God — I've come over all tired. I'm going to put my head down for a minute.
Griff Kids.
Vernon Perhaps if we go outside ——
Rita Is it just one?
Nigel No, you're all right where you are.
Griff Oh, yes.
Vernon It's best if I go.
Rita Me too.
Nigel Just stay where you are ...
Ruby Let him go. I'll stay here with you.
Nigel No, he wants to be here. You do, don't you, Vern?

Nigel and Ruby look at Vernon. He smiles rather uncomfortably

Nigel snuggles down into the bed. Ruby straightens the blankets around him then sits next to the bed. During the following she strokes the back of Nigel's hand. Vernon just looks on

Rita Is he going to be all right?
Griff He'll be home by the weekend, but I don't know that he'll ever be right.

Vernon moves to look out of the window in the door

Rita Oh, I'm sorry.

Griff Not half as much as I am.

Rita (*after a slight pause*) My son's in a coma. He was involved in an accident. (*She begins to get upset*) He hasn't come round yet.

Ruby Him and his father had a bit of a to-do on Saturday.

Vernon I know. He told me about it.

Ruby That's just like him — typical of him. He's like an open book.

Griff (*not really sure what to say or how to handle the situation*) He's going to be all right though, is he? Your boy?

Rita (*trying to pull herself together*) I lost him once, I can't lose him again.

Vernon You know, I'm surprised we haven't met before.

Ruby I'm not. Nigel keeps that side of his life away from his father. Griff has only just found out. He's still coming to terms with it. How did you take it?

Griff You on your own?

Rita My husband's here somewhere.

Ruby I bet you were sympathetic. You look the sympathetic type to me.

Vernon I was supportive, yes.

Griff When you say you lost him ... your boy now, I mean ——

Rita He went away.

Ruby That's a good word, supportive.

Rita Disappeared.

Ruby That sums it up about right, that does. Supportive.

Rita We didn't hear anything from him for thirteen months.

Ruby I wish to God our Griff could find it in himself to be that.

Griff How did you get him back?

Vernon If he's only just found out then you've got to give him time.

Ruby That's exactly what I said to him out there.

Rita He just got in touch.

Ruby You've got to give yourself time, I said. It'll all come right in the end.

Rita He got himself together and he got in touch.

Ruby That's what I keep telling myself, anyway, but none of us know what's round the corner see, do we?

Vernon looks at Ruby, but doesn't answer her

Rita When he came home he had a whole set of new problems but me and Vernon, that's my husband, we didn't care. He was back and that's all that mattered.

Griff (*after a slight pause in which he gets up and wanders down R*) I didn't want my son to go either. Oh, he didn't just disappear like yours. His year away was all planned. London. (*A slight pause*) Did yours go to ... ?

Rita Yes.

Griff They all seem to bugger off there, don't they? (*A slight pause*) We were never close — still not. I played it very cool. Go, I said, it'll make a man of you. I can still see his face now. I didn't really know what his expression meant, not at the time, anyway. I don't know how it would have turned out if he hadn't gone. Either way I suspect things would have stayed the same. (*A slight pause*) He never listened to me, it was all his mother, but I can't help wondering what would have happened if I'd said something. Would it have made any difference if I'd said, "Stay — I want you to stay." (*A slight pause*) Would you have stopped your boy if you could?

Rita I'd have tried ... His circumstances were — different, and difficult though. He really was running away. (*A slight pause*) Still, that's all behind him now. And I do believe what happened then happened for the best. And for the first time in his life, I think he's happy. He has a partner who loves him and a family who cares. What more could he want — could anyone want. I certainly wouldn't wish his past on him again.

Ruby (*still stroking Nigel's hand*) He's fast now. (*A slight pause*) You know, I try not to think about it but can you imagine what might have happened if they hadn't had that call?

Vernon Who?

Ruby The police.

Griff (*not really knowing what to say*) I'm sure he'll be all right — your boy.

Ruby (*getting up and going to Vernon*) If that man, that anonymous man, hadn't rung in, God knows how things would have turned out. I tell you, if he was here now, I'd kiss his feet.

Vernon looks very uncomfortable

Rita Your son's going home the weekend you said?

Griff nods

Ruby Do you think he'd come forward if we offered a reward?

Vernon I've no idea.

Rita You don't know how lucky you are.

Ruby We could put a hundred up. Fifty pounds each, what do you think?

Vernon It'll probably be a waste of time.

Rita (*standing and moving down* L) I feel so guilty.

Vernon And maybe he's got a reason for being discreet.

Ruby What, he doesn't want to show he was there, you mean?

Rita I wasn't there, you see.

Vernon It's possible.

Rita At home — when the call came.

Vernon And if that's the case, I doubt that a hundred pounds will flush him out.
Ruby True.
Rita (*insistently*) I should have been there.
Ruby Shame though.
Griff It's easy to blame yourself.
Ruby I'd have liked to have shook his hand and thanked him ... wouldn't you?
Vernon (*awkwardly*) Yes — who knows, you might anyway.
Rita There was no-one at home.
Ruby Do you think I could ask you a favour?

Vernon looks at Ruby

Rita Vernon was out on business.
Ruby Oh, not now. Griff's gone so it's pointless now, but — well, the truth is, I think you're marvellous.
Rita And I had a night out ... with the girls.
Ruby You're so — well, I don't know how to put it — in control. (*She flicks her thumb up from a fist of fingers*) Get it? (*She does it again*) You know, the gas advert.

Vernon smiles slightly and nods

God knows I've tried putting things across to him but it's like talking to a brick wall.
Vernon Nigel?
Ruby (*shaking her head*) No, Griff.
Rita I didn't say who I was with so Vernon couldn't get in touch.
Ruby And I'm sure we could make some progress if he'd meet him half-way and open up a bit.
Vernon Griff?
Ruby No, Nigel!
Rita The truth is, I'm being punished.
Griff Oh, I don't think so.
Ruby I can help out there though. I've always been able to get through to him, but Griff ... well, I was beginning to think he was a lost cause.
Vernon Until when?
Ruby Until you came into it.
Rita I should have changed my job.
Griff What?
Ruby Do you think you could have a word with him?
Vernon Me?

Rita None of this would have happened if I'd worked somewhere else.

Vernon I don't even know him.

Griff You've lost me now.

Ruby I'm sure if he had someone to talk to. Someone in the same boat, so to speak.

Rita I hate lies and now I'm paying for them.

Griff Lies?

Ruby A couple of hours with you over a pint and I'm sure something will rub off.

Rita I suppose I was flattered to begin with.

Ruby What do you think, could you have a word?

Rita I had no idea where it would lead to.

Vernon What would Nigel say?

Ruby (*going to him, confidentially*) Oh, I don't think we should tell him.

Griff Are you trying to tell me what I think you're trying to tell me?

Ruby If he thought for one minute that we were involved it would put the mockers on it good and proper.

Rita Me and Vernon have our problems it's true ——

Ruby And the same would go for Griff for that matter.

Rita But we should have worked at the marriage not drifted apart.

Ruby No. This is our little secret, right? Not a word to no-one, that's my advice.

Rita You think I'm awful, don't you?

Ruby (*looking over to Nigel*) Ahh — he's resting lovely now. If you want to nip out and check on Kevin.

Vernon Yes, all right. (*He makes to leave*)

Nigel stirs

On the other hand, his mother's with him.

Ruby What are you afraid of?

Vernon I'm not afraid of anything.

Ruby What does Nigel know that I don't?

Griff (*taking Rita's cup*) Have another cup of coffee ... I am.

Ruby You haven't answered me.

Rita Do you think I should say something?

Griff (*moving to the coffee machine*) To who?

Ruby (*having an idea*) Perhaps someone else knows about it.

Rita Vernon.

Vernon Someone else?

Griff Your husband?

Vernon Like who?

Ruby Your wife. (*She heads for the door*)

Vernon No, look — don't do that.
Griff What would you want to tell him about?
Vernon (*moving away down* c) I've been a bit of a naughty boy.
Rita (*moving away down* c) My affair.
Griff (*after a slight pause*) What would be the point of that?
Ruby I knew there was something.
Rita It's not too late to be honest. Maybe if I come clean, Kevin will take a turn for the better.
Griff I don't think it works like that.
Vernon Nigel found out.
Rita So you don't think I should say anything then?
Griff I'm a guard with British Rail. I'm not a Marriage Guidance Counsellor.
Vernon To be honest, I'm not sure what he's going to do about it.
Rita I just thought you could help. Sometimes it's better talking to a stranger.
Ruby You think he might say something to your wife?
Griff I don't know what to tell you.
Rita I feel so guilty, advise me.
Vernon I think there's every possibility of it.
Griff I don't think I would even if I knew what to say.
Ruby But why? Why would Nigel want to do that to you?
Vernon It's a long story.
Rita If I thought it would do Kevin any good, I would tell Vernon everything.
Griff Everything?
Rita Yes. You know, who, when, where, how long it's been going on for ...
Griff I don't think that would benefit anyone really, do you?
Rita (*after a slight pause*) Maybe not — except me. Maybe I'm looking to get the whole thing off my chest.
Griff Well, you have in a way — you've told me. (*He holds out a cup of coffee to Rita*)
Rita Yes. (*She takes the coffee*)

Griff sits

The one good thing about talking to a stranger is that at least there's not going to be any recriminations. (*She sits next to him*) I mean, it's highly unlikely that we'll ever see each other again after today — or after the weekend anyway, once your son ... I'm sorry what did you say his name was?
Griff Nigel.
Rita (*after a slight pause*) Nigel. (*A slight pause*) Nigel?
Griff Nigel.
Rita Oh my God!
Vernon You don't know this but Kevin and Nigel are splitting up.

Griff What's the matter?
Ruby What? No way — I don't believe it.
Vernon It's true.
Rita I've just realized who you are.
Vernon Nigel told me.
Griff Do I know you?
Ruby He hasn't said a word to me and he tells me everything.
Rita You have to promise me you won't say anything.
Griff To who?
Vernon Wake him up and ask him if you don't believe me.
Rita Nigel.
Griff About what?
Ruby They've had a row, I expect; it's nothing that won't blow over.
Rita Me and Peter.
Griff Who the hell is Peter?
Rita My boss.
Vernon No, I think there's more to it than that.

During the following, Ruby holds Nigel's hand and strokes his hair

Griff You've lost me again now. Why would I tell Nigel about you and your boss?
Rita You don't know who I am, do you?
Griff Should I?
Rita I'm Rita. (*A slight pause*) Rita. Vernon's wife.
Griff Vernon?
Rita Kevin's father.
Griff That might help if I knew who Kevin was.
Rita Kevin. Kevin.
Griff Kevin.
Rita Nigel and Kevin.
Griff (*after a slight pause*) Oh ... (*The penny drops*) Oh hell. (*He gets up and moves away downstage*)
Ruby Kevin is everything to Nigel. I hope he's not going to hurt him.
Vernon I think the best thing is not to get involved.
Ruby Oh, I couldn't do that. I've stood by him all his life ... I couldn't stand aside now. And you shouldn't either if what you say about them is right.
Vernon It's a bit more complicated than that.
Ruby No, it's not — it's simple ... (*she gets up and moves downstage*) ... if they have a tiff and turn to us, all we have to do is turn them back to each other. They'll sort it all out. It's like my mother used to say to me, "You've made your bed now go and lie on it".
Vernon But Kevin doesn't want to lie on it. Not that bed anyway. He doesn't want to live that kind of life any more.

Ruby Well, bully for him.
Vernon You know he used to be married. You did know, didn't you?

Ruby nods

According to Nigel he wants to give it another shot. I'm not sure why ...
There's a child involved. Maybe it's got something to do with her.
Ruby Well, knowing Nigel, he won't give up — not without a fight.
Vernon (*sighing*) Yes. I'd say you know him very well in that case.
Ruby And I'll be standing there right next to him too.
Vernon You really should let them get on with it.
Ruby No, indeed I'm not. I'm going to help him get as much ammunition as I can.
Vernon That's what I was afraid of.
Ruby No-one hurts my boy and gets away with it.
Vernon Look, can I make a deal with you?

Rita gets up and joins Griff

Griff What sort of a deal?
Rita I don't know. I just don't want you to say anything.
Ruby To who?
Vernon To Rita.
Rita To Vernon.
Griff It's none of my business.
Ruby What's it worth to keep my mouth shut?
Rita That's very good of you.
Vernon You're going to have to gag Nigel as well.
Griff No it's not. I just don't want to get involved.
Ruby It's not going to be easy. What's in it for me?
Vernon (*meaning Nigel*) Well, it's for him really.
Ruby For him then?
Rita If there's anything I can do in return.
Vernon I told Nigel I'd stand by Kevin in his decision to leave ...
Ruby You'd support him you mean?
Vernon Yes—but if Rita's kept from hearing where I was on Saturday, then I'll stand back and be impartial.
Griff The best thing to do is to forget all about it.
Ruby Not good enough. To keep your little secret safe I want you to encourage them to stay together.
Rita I don't know how to thank you.
Vernon What if it doesn't work?
Ruby If it doesn't work, it doesn't work. Just promise me you'll do your best.
Rita I don't know what you must think of me.

Griff It's not for me to judge. To each his own I suppose.
Ruby (*offering Vernon her hand*) Is it a deal?
Rita (*offering Griff her hand*) Thank you.

Both couples shake hands

The Nurse comes in with a small tray. On it are some pills and a small container filled with water

Nurse It's all right for some. I haven't had a coffee since six o'clock this morning.
Griff Join us if you like.
Nurse I daren't. It's all right anyway. I go to break in half an hour.
Rita Is Kevin back yet?
Nurse Due any time. They're not usually very long. Excuse me. (*She goes into Nigel's room*)
Griff Have they taken him somewhere?
Rita He's gone for a brain scan.
Nurse (*entering the room and seeing Nigel*) My God, look at Sleeping Beauty.
Griff Tell me, what do you make of it all?
Nurse Come on, sunshine — time for your medication.

The Nurse gently wakes Nigel

Griff You know ... with the boys and that.
Nigel What did you wake me for? I was having a lovely dream.
Nurse Was I in it?
Nigel A *lovely* dream I said.
Rita It's like you said, I suppose — to each his own.
Nurse Come on — get this down your neck.
Nigel Ooooh, you've gone and broken it now.
Nurse (*shocked*) I don't believe you.
Vernon (*making to leave*) Excuse me.
Nigel Where are you going?
Vernon To the Gents.

Vernon leaves Nigel's room

Rita It does get easier.

Griff turns to look at Rita

Vernon approaches Rita

Nigel (*to the Nurse*) I need to go too. Can you get me a bottle?

The Nurse hands Nigel a bottle from the bedside cabinet. He takes it and places it between his legs under the blankets

Rita (*seeing Vernon*) Vernon. Where have you come from?
Vernon I've been in with Nigel. How's Kevin?
Rita There's no change. Vernon, this is — did you tell me your name?
Griff No ... it's ... er ... Griff.
Rita I'm Rita. Griff is Nigel's father.
Vernon I know. We were both in there together for a while.
Griff A short while. Is he still performing?
Vernon He's still Nigel if that's what you mean.
Rita Have a cup of coffee — you look like you need one. (*She moves to the machine*)
Vernon No, I'm all right ... it's the Gents I need.

Vernon exits R

Rita He hasn't taken it very well. (*She looks off R after Vernon*) He and Kevin were really close lately. They never used to get on but they've been really close lately.
Nigel It's no good. I can't do anything with you two in here.
Nurse Well, I'm not leaving. I'm going to take your blood pressure.
Nigel Again?
Ruby I'll pop out then. About five minutes is it, Nurse?
Nurse Fine.

Ruby leaves the room and enters the corridor

The Nurse takes Nigel's blood pressure during the following

Nigel I've always been the same. I've never been able to pee in front of anyone. And I can't do it in here. (*Meaning the bed*) It feels all wrong. Perhaps if I could sit in a chair?
Nurse I know what you're up to and you can forget it.
Ruby (*seeing Griff*) Griff? I thought you'd gone ages ago.
Griff Have a guess who this is.
Ruby Kevin's mother.
Griff How did you know!

Ruby I didn't. I just put two and two together. (*She moves to Rita*) How is he, all right?

Rita half smiles and shrugs

Don't worry, I'm sure he'll be fine. (*She puts her hand on Rita's arm*)

Rita looks at Ruby's hand

Griff They've sent him down for a brain scan.
Ruby Let's hope you'll never have to have one of them then.
Griff Now don't start.
Ruby I'm only making light of it. God knows it's depressing enough here as it is. (*To Rita*) Still hasn't come round yet I take it?

Rita shakes her head

I'm Ruby by the way.
Rita Rita.
Ruby You're a spit of Kevin, has anyone ever told you?
Nigel (*holding out the empty bottle to the Nurse*) You may as well have this back — it's hopeless.

The Nurse takes the bottle and places it back on the cabinet; she then leans back over Nigel to continue

Griff Do you want a cup of coffee or something?
Ruby Yes, all right, go on then.
Griff Rita?
Rita Please.

Griff obliges. Ruby stares at Rita and smiles sympathetically

Nigel If it's still normal can I sit up in a chair?
Nurse Shut up, I'm counting.
Ruby I don't like hospitals but it's a good job we got 'em, innit?

Griff is obviously having trouble with the coffee machine. He taps it a few times

Nigel You'd better say yes — you're in a very vulnerable position.
Nurse Not half as vulnerable as you are, sunshine. I've smothered many a man with these before now. (*Meaning her breasts*)

Nigel I bet you have.

Griff begins to hit hell out of the coffee machine

Ruby Don't do that.

Griff But it's not working.

Ruby You'd have enough to say if some teenager started doing that to one of your trains.

Griff There's only a load of steam coming out.

Ruby A bit like you that is then, innit? There's another machine down the corridor. Go and get it from there.

Rita (*sitting back down in one of the chairs*) Don't bother for me, I've had two already.

Ruby Nonsense. It's no bother for him. Go ahead — go on.

Griff looks at Ruby. She gestures for him to leave

Griff exits

There is a pause

Ruby sits next to Rita

There is another pause

You don't have to talk if you don't want to. I understand. Sometimes it's nice just to sit and be quiet, innit? (*Another pause*) I find that hard, I do, though. The minute someone stops talking I always feel I got to chip in, you know. (*Another pause*) You like a bit of quiet, though, I can see. (*A slight pause*) Nothing wrong in that. (*A slight pause*) If that's what you're into.

Rita You're a road-crossing patrol officer I see.

Ruby A lollipop lady, yes. It's only a couple of hours a day but it keeps me off the street. (*She laughs*) Get it? I always say that — but no-one ever laughs, only me. What do you do?

Rita I'm a PA.

Ruby (*quickly trying to work this out*) Oh ... right. Have you worked for the Borough Council long?

Rita I'm a personal assistant.

Ruby (*laughing*) Good God and there's me thinking you were a park attendant. So you're a secretary then?

Rita A personal assistant, yes.

Ruby "Take a letter Miss Jones", that sort of thing.

Rita doesn't answer

The only lap I ever sat on was Father Christmas's. And then he frightened
me so much I wet him soaking.

Rita Embarrassing.

Ruby Oh, it was — I was thirty-six at the time. (*She laughs*) I'm not normally
this chirpy you know, I'm only doing it to cheer you up.

Rita I'm sorry but I'm not in the mood.

Ruby I can see that, that's why I thought I'd try and make you laugh — or
smile. (*A slight pause*) I suppose I'd be the same if my son was — well, you
know. Still, anything can happen. Last night wasn't very good for Nigel but
today he's as right as rain. Have you been in to see him?

Rita shakes her head

No, of course you haven't. We'll go in together now. Soon as the nurse
have ——

Rita Er ... no!

Ruby What?

Rita I don't want to see him.

Ruby is shocked and just stares at Rita

Have you ever been in the car with him? Have you seen the way he drives?

Ruby (*in Nigel's defence*) Hey look, you hang on a minute, by here now. I
know you're going through hell, but you want to stop and think about what
you're saying.

Rita I'm surprised there hasn't been some sort of accident before now.

Ruby Now you've hit the nail on the head by there. *Accidents* are accidents.
I know you're in a bit of a state but ... You don't think for a minute either
of them would choose to be in here, do you?

Rita (*reluctantly*) No.

Ruby No. You know Nigel thinks the world of your Kevin — and to be
honest, I do too. (*A slight pause*) You and Kevin — are things good
between you?

Rita (*after a slight pause*) They're all right.

Ruby All right isn't the same as good — well not in my book, anyway. (*A
pause*) There was a time when I used to wonder what things would be like
if they were different — but if things were different then the boys wouldn't
be who they are, and if they weren't who they are, who's to say we would
have loved them as much?

Rita looks up at Ruby but doesn't say anything

During the following, the Nurse enters Nigel's details on to his chart

Nigel Kevin is going to be all right, isn't he?
Ruby You don't look old enough to be Kevin's mother.
Nurse I've told you all I know.
Nigel But what do you think?
Nurse I think you should stop worrying and rest up.
Nigel I can't. Not while Kev's like he is.
Ruby Had him young did you?
Nigel (*after a slight pause*) Perhaps later on ... when everyone's gone home you'll take me in?

The Nurse doesn't answer

Rita I was twenty-three.
Nigel I've got to see him. I need to.

The Nurse still doesn't commit herself

Ruby And what's Kevin now — twenty-four, twenty-five?
Nigel I've got to tell him I'm sorry.
Rita Twenty-four.
Nurse For causing the accident?
Ruby (*doing a quick mental addition*) You're forty-seven then.
Nigel It wasn't an accident.
Nurse (*after a slight pause*) What?
Ruby I was twenty-nine having Nigel.
Nigel I was so upset.
Ruby I'm fifty- (*she mouths*) five now.
Nigel He was saying terrible things.
Nurse You mean you crashed the car on purpose?
Ruby It's hard to believe that there's nine years between us, innit?
Nigel The last thing I remember thinking was, if I couldn't have him, she wasn't going to.
Ruby Bit of a career woman, are you?
Nurse Do you realize what you're saying?
Nigel I've got to tell someone or I think I'll go crazy.
Ruby I've never had any ambition myself.
Nigel I didn't think it would turn out like this. I thought we would both die together.
Ruby I didn't work at all until this little number came along.
Nurse Look, I didn't hear what you just said, right? If anything went wrong with Kevin you could be in deep shit.
Nigel Why do you think I need to know that he's going to be all right?

Ruby It was my friend's job really. She asked me to cover for her while she went to visit her daughter in Australia and she never came back. I didn't know she had died till they sent her ashes home.

Nigel You should see our act.

Nurse Maybe I will.

Nigel Yeah ... (*A slight pause*). And maybe you won't.

Ruby Have you ever been to Australia?

Rita shakes her head

No, or me.

Nigel We're very good, you know.

Nurse I bet you are.

Nigel We could get somewhere if we really pushed it. (*A pause*) He still loved me, he said ... (*He becomes upset, crying quietly, his head forward*)

The Nurse puts her arm around Nigel's shoulders

There is a slight pause. Ruby looks at Rita and smiles. She might even touch Rita's hand

Ruby He's going to be all right, I'm sure he is. And it's like I said ... no-one's to blame. Believe me love, it's the easiest thing in the world to point a finger.

Vernon enters

Vernon Kevin's back.

Rita What?

Vernon In his room. He's back.

Rita (*standing*) Right.

Vernon No, don't go, yet. They're still making him comfortable.

Ruby Now's your chance to pop in and see Nigel.

Rita Yes.

Vernon No! Er — on the other hand, they've probably finished with Kevin by now.

Ruby (*to Rita*) Go in and see Nigel first, go on. Two minutes — you won't be long.

Rita goes into Nigel's room. Ruby makes to follow her but stops briefly to have a quick and quiet word with Vernon

Don't worry. I'll see that nothing's said. (*She enters Nigel's room*) All right, Nurse?

Nurse (*to Nigel*) You've got visitors.

Ruby Look who's come to see you.

Nigel (*seeing Rita*) Rita. (*He quickly hides his tears*)

Rita Before you say anything, I did blame you, but I know that's not going to get us anywhere.

Vernon stands outside Nigel's room, pondering. He then goes to the coffee machine and has a drink without any problem whatsoever

Nigel I'm sorry. It should never have happened.

Nurse It's a perfectly natural reaction after an RTA. I call it the "if only syndrome". "If only I did this" and "if only I did that".

Rita I don't want you blaming yourself. It's like your mother said — it was an accident.

Nigel But what if Kevin ——

Nurse Look, I'm not really a religious person, but do you know what we often do on the wards in situations like these? We all hold hands and close our eyes together.

Rita Pray, you mean?

Nurse You can call it a prayer if you want to. I just think it helps sometimes to concentrate and think about the person we want to get well. You might even feel better for it yourself.

Ruby It definitely sounds like a prayer to me. What do you say, Reet?

Nurse Come on. Shall we do it or what?

Rita (*after a slight pause*) Why not.

The Nurse holds out both her arms and everyone in the room hesitantly joins hands

Nurse Now close your eyes.

They all look at each other then eventually close their eyes

A pause

> *Griff enters the corridor from* R, *carrying two coffees. He stops when he sees Vernon*

Griff We haven't met properly. Vernon, innit? (*He offers his hand but it's holding a coffee. He offers his other hand but that has a coffee in it as well. He places both cups on top of the coffee machine*)

Vernon Vernon.

They shake hands

Griff (*after a slight pause*) Bit of a circus all this, isn't it?

Vernon (*after a slight pause*) Is it me or has it gone very quiet in there? (*Meaning Nigel's room*)

Griff I can't handle it myself.

Vernon What?

Griff You know — Nigel and — er — Kevin. (*A pause*) You cope all right, do you?

Vernon I don't think too much about it. Especially now with Kevin ...

Griff Of course. (*A pause*) Have you known long?

Vernon About the boys?

Griff nods

> Right from the start or just about.

Griff moves away and nods his head several more times

Vernon I know about Saturday.

Griff What?

Vernon Nigel told me what he did. I know it must have been awful for you but try not to take it out on him. He's hurting. I know you are too, but — don't make the same mistake I did.

Griff The truth is I don't like him very much. What mistake did *you* make?

Vernon I tried to change him. Well, I encouraged it which is much the same thing.

Griff Do you blame yourself for how he turned out?

Vernon I did for a while, then the more I thought about it the more common sense took and explained it. It's no-one's fault.

Griff So you don't think anything could, you know — influence them then.

Vernon No, not in either way. (*A slight pause*) That wasn't always the case, though. I remember in the beginning, when we first found out, I was looking for all kinds of reasons and people to blame. (*A slight pause*) The three of us went on a trip to Blackpool once. Kevin must have only been about eight. There was this dick-head on the bus who dressed up in a wig and a frock and I know I blamed him for a while.

For a moment Griff doesn't know where to look

Vernon Things haven't always been good between Kevin and me. We've both made mistakes but thank God we've been big enough to learn by them.

Griff So you accept him now?

Vernon You'll be surprised what you'll accept when you view the alternative. It depends on how you feel I suppose — and what you're prepared to let stand in the way.

The Nurse opens her eyes

Nurse There you are then.

The others open their eyes

Vernon You know, it's definitely gone quiet in there. (*He looks through the door windows*)

Griff looks thoughtful through the following scene

Nurse That was all right, wasn't it? Now I'm going to have to go. Duty calls.
Ruby Thank you, Nurse.
Rita Yes, thank you.
Nigel Let's hope it'll do some good.
Nurse I feel better for it already.
Ruby I didn't like to say anything but *I* feel different too.

Vernon comes to sit down on one of the chairs

Nigel You're all right are you, Mam? The old man's got enough on his plate with *me* without having you see the light.
Ruby I just feel — nice. Do you know what I mean, Reet? I can't explain it really ... but it's like a big cloud has just passed over and I feel all nice and warm.

Griff sits next to Vernon

Nigel (*meaning Ruby's coat*) I'm not surprised you're hot in that thing.
Ruby You can make fun if you like.
Nurse And he will.
Ruby (*to Rita*) What about you, Reet? Can't you feel it?
Rita Not really.
Nigel I don't think it's God, I think it's the change of life.
Ruby I've never had a flush like this before.
Nigel That sounds like a cue for a song.
Nurse No, it's my cue to go.
Ruby You don't have to run, I'm not going to sing.

Nurse (*playfully*) There are other patients on this ward besides your son, you
know.

The Nurse goes into the corridor

Ruby (*meaning the Nurse*) Smashin' girl.
Nurse (*seeing Griff and Vernon*) Everything all right?
Vernon (*standing*) Yes ... what about in there?
Nurse Fine.
Vernon (*after a slight pause*) Kevin's back. I'm just going to go and see him.
(*He makes to leave*)
Nurse Good, I'll come with you.

Vernon leads off and the Nurse follows him

Vernon exits

*The Nurse is almost out of sight when she stops, turns and comes back to
speak to Griff*

Nigel There's something I've got to tell you.
Nurse Still here then. I thought you'd have gone ages ago.
Griff Just going. (*He doesn't move. A pause. He eventually moves to pick
up his bag*)
Rita I want to know what happened and I want to know why.

*During the following, Nigel tells Rita, in mime, what happened in the car and
why*

Nurse You can tell me to mind my own business if you like ——
Griff Mind your own business.
Rita (*to Nigel*) How long has he been seeing her?
Nurse I can see you don't get on, you and Nigel. You remind me of me and
my father.
Griff You don't know what you're talking about.
Nurse He's a very proud man, too.
Griff Leave it there now, will you? I don't want to talk about it.
Nurse But you should. All right perhaps not to me but you should talk about
it.
Rita (*to Nigel*) And you knew nothing about it?
Nurse He chucked me out, my father. I was seventeen. I got myself into
trouble and he couldn't cope with the shame. (*A slight pause*) I had a little
girl. You should see them together now.
Griff It's not the same thing at all.

Nurse Of course it is.
Griff He's nothing to me. There was never much between us before but it's all gone now.
Nurse That's pride talking.
Griff I'm telling you. I can't bear to look at him.
Nurse Because you're hurt.
Griff Because I'm ashamed.
Rita Why did he tell you in the car?
Nurse You won't admit it but you're closer than you think.
Griff No.
Nurse You're a proud man, Mr Gregory.
Griff He's broken me.
Nurse Then pick up the pieces and start again.
Griff I can't.
Nurse You mean you don't want to.
Griff I mean I can't.
Rita (*her attitude changing*) Are you're saying it wasn't an accident?
Ruby (*defending Nigel*) Don't take any notice of him, he don't know what he's saying.
Nurse I know you're ashamed and pride is a terrible thing, but it's only there shielding your hurt. I know it sounds corny, but it's true, you know. You can hurt the ones you love and the ones who love you back.
Griff You think Nigel's hurting.
Nurse More than you know.

Nigel is now upset

Rita (*outraged and upset*) Suicide?
Ruby He's delirious, that's what he is. He's talking a load of nonsense.
Nurse And if you don't put things right, or meet him half-way, or do something, then you'll never know. (*A slight pause*) Do you know what my little girl asked me last week? She asked me if a caterpillar could love a butterfly — and the answer to that is: why not? (*A slight pause*) Right. That's my little speech over. I'm off now to clean bedpans.

The Nurse exits R

Griff is left just standing there

Nigel So you see it's all my fault.
Ruby No!
Nigel If anyone should be in a coma it's me.
Ruby Don't say that.
Rita If anything happens to Kevin, I'll never forgive you.

Ruby Now nothing's going to happen to him, right? (*A slight pause*) I'm going to get something to drink. Anything for you, Reet?

Rita doesn't reply

How about a nice cup of tea ... if I can coax one out of the machine. Nigel?
Nigel No.

Ruby goes out into the corridor and sees Griff still standing there

Ruby Well, you're a fine one, you are.
Nigel Try and understand how I felt.
Ruby I send you off for coffee and I don't see you for quarter of an hour.
Griff They're there, look. (*He points to the two coffees on top of the machine*)
Ruby We don't want 'em now, we're having tea instead. (*She helps herself at the machine*)
Nigel I panicked and over-reacted.
Ruby What time do you start work?
Griff I'm just leaving.
Nigel I must have been out of my head.

Ruby can't get anything out of the machine and kicks it in frustration. There is a slight pause

Ruby He didn't really mean it, you know.
Griff Shut up, I don't want to hear.
Nigel I didn't mean to hurt him — you do realize that, don't you?
Ruby Emotionally, he's all over the shop.
Griff (*shouting*) Shut up, I said! I'm sick of everyone making excuses for him. I've had a gutsful of people telling me to give him time, to give *myself* time — I've had enough. Enough, right? I don't want to hear stories about caterpillars and butterflies.
Ruby Caterpillars and bloody butterflies? Who the hell have *you* been talking to?

Vernon rushes on suddenly. We shouldn't be able to tell from his initial reaction whether he is anxious or excited

Vernon Where's Rita?
Ruby (*pointing to Nigel's room*) What is it? What's wrong?
Vernon It's Kevin.

Vernon rushes into Nigel's room and Ruby and Griff follow

Vernon (*to Rita*) Come quick, it's Kevin.
Rita (*thinking the worst*) Oh, my God!
Vernon No, it's all right. It's all right, he's opened his eyes. He did. He
opened his eyes and spoke to me.
Rita What did he say?
Vernon (*after a slight pause*) He said — he said: "Where's Nige?"

There is a slight pause

Rita and Vernon rush into the corridor followed quickly by Ruby

*The Nurse enters the corridor from the opposite direction and sees all the
commotion*

Nurse What's happening?
Ruby (*without stopping*) It's Kevin. He's come round.

Rita, Vernon and Ruby exit; the Nurse rushes off after them

Griff is left alone with Nigel

There is a pause

*Nigel is obviously very emotional about Kevin and is drying his face with his
hands*

A long pause

Griff Good news then I suppose.

Another pause

Nigel What are you doing here?
Griff I'm not apologizing.
Nigel Neither am I.
Griff That's all right then.
Nigel So what are you doing here?
Griff I'm with your mother.
Nigel She's in with Kevin.
Griff You want me to go?
Nigel You can please yourself.
Griff All right, I'll go then. (*A slight pause*) That's fair enough. (*Another
pause*) You're not going to stop me, are you?

Nigel No.

A pause. Griff turns to leave

What do you want from me?
Griff Oh, I can't have that.
Nigel There's lots of things *I* can't have either.
Griff Do you have any idea what you did to me Saturday night?
Nigel Yes — but that was nothing to what you've done to me all my life.
Griff It hasn't been easy for me.
Nigel You think *I've* had an easy ride? *(A slight pause)* I've been to hell and
back to get where I am — but I am what I am and I'm damned if I'm going
to apologize for it. *(A slight pause)* Don't tell me how hard it's been for you.
Where were you when I didn't know what I was ... *who* I was? Eh? *(He
shouts)* I was an only child for Christ's sake! Who could *I* turn to? You
couldn't talk to me about the weather, let alone the facts of life! *(He starts
to laugh but the laughter is tinged with tears)* Do you remember me asking
you what a wank was?

Griff doesn't answer

"Ask your mother," you said. *(Shouting)* "Ask your mother", and you
wonder why I turned to her ...
Griff I haven't been a bad father.
Nigel No ... you've been a *very* bad father. *(A slight pause)* "What's a wank,
Mam?" I said. Do you know what she told me? "It's the opposite to a wink."
(Shouting) "It's the opposite to a wink," she said, "now shut up and eat your
Weetabix."
Griff *(after a pause, quietly)* I'm sorry.
Nigel What's that, I didn't hear it?
Griff *(shouting)* I said I'm sorry!

There is a pause

Nigel Yeah ... me and you both. I don't know that we'll ever get it right ...
but for what it's worth, I wish I hadn't done what I did on Saturday. I can't
apologize for it but I wish I hadn't done it.
Griff *(after a slight pause)* I suppose there's a lot we both can't apologize
for ... your costumes for one thing.
Nigel You mean my dresses?
Griff I was angry.
Nigel What are you saying?
Griff I got rid of them.

Nigel (*after a slight pause*) It was some sort of symbolic gesture, no doubt.
Griff I don't know what it was.
Nigel Probably deep down in your subconscious you were getting rid of me.
(*A slight pause*) Yes, well — we seem to be stuck with each other no matter
what, don't we?
Griff I still don't like what you do — what you are.
Nigel I still haven't forgiven you for it.
Griff So you blame me.
Nigel I blame you for lots of things.
Griff (*after a slight pause*) So where do we go from here?
Nigel I don't know.
Griff We must be making some progress. I thought you'd flip when I told
you about the dresses.
Nigel (*shaking his head, then smiling*) I've got twenty more in the house. (*A
pause*) Who's Ritchie Thomas?
Griff (*on the defensive*) What do you want to know about him for?
Nigel I heard you and the old girl talking about him, that's all.
Griff He was a mate ... (*he corrects himself*) ... a friend. (*He moves around
to the other side of the bed*)
Nigel Why haven't I heard of him before?
Griff We grew up together. He's been dead for years.
Nigel What did he die of?
Griff Why do you want to know?
Nigel (*raising his voice a little*) I just want to know what he died of.
Griff What difference does it make?
Nigel (*shouting*) Tell me what he died of!
Griff Mind your own bloody business!

A pause

> *Ruby comes into the corridor followed by the Nurse who is pushing an
> empty wheelchair. They are on their way to Nigel's room*

Ruby I wonder if that little prayer or whatever it was had anything to do with
it, Nurse?
Nurse Who's to say? It might have even been that little trip to the scanner
and back.
Ruby I reckon there's a bit more to it than that.

The Nurse and Ruby enter Nigel's room

Nurse (*to Nigel*) Guess where you're going!

Nigel Home?

Nurse Not quite. There's someone in a room down the corridor that's desperate to see you.

Nigel (*smiling*) How is he doing?

Nurse You'll see for yourself in a minute. You won't be able to stay long though, he's got to be checked over by the house doctors who are probably on their way as we speak, so it's just a quick in and out, all right?

Nigel Sometimes they're the best.

Nurse Naughty.

The Nurse gets Nigel into the wheelchair and begins to wheel him out

Nigel (*as he goes*) You will be here when I get back, Mam?

Ruby Yes.

Griff I don't think I will.

Nigel and Griff stare at each other for a moment

Nigel (*to the Nurse*) Come on.

They move into the corridor, heading for the exit

There is a pause

Griff and Ruby look at each other before she looks away

Griff What?

Ruby (*looking back at Griff*) What?

Griff You may as well say it.

Ruby What?

Griff What you were going to say.

Ruby I wasn't going to say anything.

Griff You've got something on your mind.

There is a slight pause. Ruby looks away and shakes her head

Nigel (*to the Nurse*) Wait a minute.

Nigel and the Nurse stop in the corridor

Griff It's no good.

Nigel Will he remember anything?

Ruby What isn't?

Griff Me and Nigel.

Nigel About Saturday. The crash.
Griff Too much water's gone under the bridge.
Nurse I'm not sure. It's possible.

The Nurse and Nigel exit

Ruby You've talked to him then?
Griff It was a waste of time.
Ruby I could have told you that.
Griff What?
Ruby Look, the only way you can make any headway with Nigel is to be honest with him — and how can you do that when you can't even be honest with yourself.
Griff *(after a slight pause)* All this with him ... he thinks it's my fault, he told me.
Ruby Griff, can't you see what he's doing? He's trying to make you feel guilty, responsible, because the minute you start taking some of the blame, he'll start taking it from you.
Griff Don't be ridiculous.
Ruby *(sitting on the R edge of the bed)* He will, believe me, he will. Trust me. Work it out together. *(A slight pause)* It's a big job and it's not going to happen overnight. It's going to take time — maybe the rest of your life — but don't give up on him, Griff. It's going to be a long hard slog, but don't give up on him — that would be easy — and if you can't do it for him, perhaps you'll do it for me.

Griff looks at Ruby. There is a slight pause. He can't promise anything

Griff I wish we could go back and do it all over again.
Ruby What would be the point of that?
Griff I wouldn't make the same mistakes.
Ruby No, you'd make different ones. Don't be too hard on yourself. You can't go through life without putting one foot wrong.
Griff You don't blame me then?
Ruby Nobody gets it dead right, Griff. Not me, you or Nigel.

Griff stares at Ruby for a moment

Anyway, whatever you decide to do I want you to take it easy on him for a bit. He's going through a bad patch at the moment and he's going to need all the support he can get.
Griff Support?
Ruby Yes. If you don't know what it means, have a word with Vernon.

Griff You want me to take a leaf out of *his* book?
Ruby A paragraph would be nice.
Griff It must be marvellous to get it right.
Ruby No-one ever does — not the first time, anyway. You've got to be prepared to get it wrong.
Griff I'm half-way there then.
Ruby What I'm saying, Griff, is that it's all right to get it wrong providing you hang on in there and try again. Of course you've got to *want* to do it — and you've got to do it yourself. And it's got to come from in there. (*She taps him on the chest*)

Rita and Vernon come on from R

Vernon ... it's routine. They want to have a look at him, you know, give him the once over, just to confirm everything's all right.
Rita Yes ... we've got him back, that's the main thing.
Vernon But will Nigel, that's the question.
Rita (*after a slight pause*) What do you think about it all?
Vernon I don't know. You?
Rita It's difficult, isn't it? The temptation is to charge in and get them to do what you think is best ... but we both know that's not the answer, don't we?

Vernon doesn't reply

All we can do is be there for both of them.
Vernon To pat them on the back?
Rita Or pick up the pieces. We shouldn't get involved, that's what I'm saying.
Vernon What if they ask us to?
Rita We're still making our own mistakes ... I think we should let them get on with it. The whole thing could blow over and we could be left taking sides.
Vernon So we leave things as they are, is that what you're saying? (*She doesn't answer him*)
Rita (*after a slight pause*) This morning I wanted two things more than anything else in the world. The first was for Kevin to open his eyes ...
Vernon And the second?
Rita (*after a slight pause*) I want to change my job.
Vernon What?
Rita I'm going to change my job.
Vernon Why now, all of a sudden? Has it got something to do with Kevin?
Rita It's got nothing to do with Kevin.
Vernon (*after a slight pause*) Well ... if you're sure it's what you want.

Rita It's what I want, yes.

The Nurse enters wheeling Nigel in his wheelchair. He is leaning on the arm of the wheelchair holding his head in one hand. The Nurse takes Nigel into his room, rolling her eyes at Vernon and Rita as she goes. Something is wrong

Ruby (*seeing Nigel*) Good God, that was quick.
Nigel It was long enough.

Vernon and Rita follow the Nurse and Nigel into the room

Ruby What's the matter?
Nurse Kevin started to get upset so it was better I took him away. (*Meaning Nigel*)
Rita Upset?
Nigel He told me to piss off, that's what she means.
Nurse (*to Nigel*) I wouldn't pay too much attention. I've told you — he's going to be totally zonked for a day or two.
Nigel Zonked my arse. He remembers everything. He hates my guts 'cos he remembers everything.
Nurse Believe me, things will be different tomorrow. Give him time to calm down and think about things.

The Nurse gets Nigel back into bed

Ruby, Griff, Rita and Vernon all look at each other awkwardly

Vernon (*after a slight pause*) It's difficult to know what to say now, isn't it?
Ruby I think we should leave them to sort it out themselves.
Griff Sort what out?
Rita Yes, the last thing they want is any interference from us.
Griff Who?
Vernon They won't thank us for it in the end.
Griff What are you talking about?
Rita I've never liked anyone sticking their nose in my business.
Ruby Or mine.
Rita So it would be wrong for us to start doing it now.
Griff (*shouting*) Doing what! Doing what! What the hell is everybody talking about?
Rita Nigel and Kevin.
Griff What about them?
Ruby Don't waste your breath now, Reet. I'll fill Griff in with all the details later.

Griff What's all this secrecy? I hate all this secrecy.
Nurse Well, you're just going to have to learn to live with it.
Griff What?
Nurse Along with a lot of other things. Am I right, Nige? Secrets are what makes the world go round. I bet all of us in this room knows at least one.

Rita, Vernon, Griff and Ruby all look very uncomfortable

Vernon (*to Rita*) Do you think we'd better go and have another look at Kevin?
Rita Yes.
Nurse They won't let you see him. The doctor will be with him by now.
Vernon We're going to have to make a move, anyway.
Rita Yes.
Griff And I need to go to work.

Rita, Vernon and Griff head for the exit

Nigel What about me?

Rita, Vernon and Griff stop

Kevin's going to be all right but where does that leave me?

No-one answers

Do any of you care?

No-one answers

Before you go — before all of you go — I've got a couple of things I want to say.
Nurse I'll be back in a minute.

The Nurse exits

Nigel Rita. Better the devil you know.
Rita What does that mean?
Nigel It means ... better the devil you know. Vern? I *am* your devil. I'm going to be on your shoulder twenty-four hours a day.

Vernon and Rita leave the room; during the following dialogue they head for the R exit

Rita (*out in the corridor*) What did he mean by that?
Vernon No idea.
Rita Do you think it was a dig at me?
Vernon No, I think it was a dig at *me*.
Rita Well *my* conscience is clear.
Vernon So's mine.

They disappear off R

Griff (*after a slight pause*) You got anything you want to say to me?
Nigel No. I've got a question for you though. (*A slight pause*) How did he
die?

Griff doesn't answer

Ruby Who you talking about?
Nigel Ritchie Thomas.
Ruby How do you know about him?
Nigel I might have got a cracked rib but I'm not deaf.

Griff points at Ruby as if to blame her

And who is he? Why haven't I heard of him before?
Ruby He was a friend of his. (*She points with her thumb to Griff*)
Nigel (*to Ruby*) Tell me about him.
Ruby Griff?

Griff shakes his head slightly

I'll tell you again. Now isn't the time.
Nigel Was he my father?

Griff almost chokes on his own spittle

Ruby What?
Nigel You heard.
Ruby What makes you think that?
Nigel I don't — but a lot of things would make sense if he was.
Ruby Well he wasn't. Believe me, Nigel, he wasn't.
Nigel Tell me how he died then.
Ruby He was a very sad man — he was lonely — confused. (*A slight pause*)
He committed suicide.

A pause

Griff It's time to go.
Nigel (*to Ruby*) And you?

Ruby nods

    Will I see you later?
Ruby Yes ... of course you will.
Nigel (*to Griff*) What about you?
Griff I don't know ... you might ... yes, all right.

Griff leaves the room and waits for Ruby outside in the corridor. Ruby stands just inside the door

A slight pause

Nigel You're sure now?
Ruby About what?
Nigel (*after a slight pause*) My father.
Ruby (*after staring at him for a moment*) I'll be back about five. (*She turns and leaves the room. She sees Griff waiting for her*)
Griff I thought we'd walk out together.

Ruby nods. A slight pause

    It's possible, isn't it?

Ruby looks at Griff

    He could be his father.
Ruby In a funny kind of way it would be a lot easier for you if he was, wouldn't it?
Griff Oh, I don't know — it would only be swapping one humiliation for another.
Ruby So it wouldn't be easier?
Griff I didn't say that.
Ruby If he wasn't your son, that would relieve you of a lot of things. It would be all right for you to feel how you do about him then because he wouldn't be your own flesh and blood.
Griff (*after a slight pause*) It's a funny thing: over the years, through all that's happened, I've always thought of him as mine.
Ruby Good.

Griff He felt mine.

Ruby (*reassuringly*) Then he is yours ...

Griff I want the truth.

Ruby No you don't, you couldn't handle it — not yet.

Griff When then?

Ruby I don't know, but I *will* know — and you and Nigel will too, when the time comes.

Griff What's going to happen until then?

Ruby shrugs. There is a slight pause

Ruby Well, hopefully, we'll live a bit, probably we'll die a bit, and with a bit of luck we might even come out of this and grow old together. All of us.

Ruby slips her arm under Griff's and they walk off

The Nurse appears from the same side as they have left and enters Nigel's room

Nurse Everybody gone?

He doesn't answer. A slight pause

Are you all right?

Nigel Oh yeah, I'm the proverbial bouncing bloody ball, me.

Nurse Are you going to be OK?

Nigel Well, I always have been before. And I've got my old girl — she's always been there for me. It can't be easy being parents.

Nurse (*sitting in the chair next to the bed*) Tell me about it.

Nigel I haven't made it easy for them.

Nurse It never is easy. If there's anything I can do for you — you know, whatever ... you've only got to ask.

Nigel Thanks.

The Nurse makes to leave

I wonder what sort of parent I would have made.

Nurse That sounds very much like you're never going to find out.

Nigel Well, I mean I'm not, am I?

Nurse You never know what's round the corner.

Nigel Dream on, sister.

Nurse You don't. Anything can happen.

Nigel I've missed *my* chance — I'm losing Kevin *and* little Kate.
Nurse So you're giving up?

Nigel doesn't answer

   I thought you had more spunk than that.
Nigel Yeah ... I thought so too. (*A slight pause*) She spends a lot of time with
   us. She likes me ... It was so easy to think of her as mine.

There is a slight pause; the Nurse stands behind the chair, leaning on it

Nurse He's a lovely looking fella — Kevin. I'm buggered if I'd give him up
   without a fight.

The Nurse looks at Nigel and smiles, then winks and leaves

Nigel is left to ponder on the advice. Music plays as ——

                    the CURTAIN *falls*

FURNITURE AND PROPERTY LIST

ACT I
SCENE 1

On stage: Four chairs
Coffee machine (practical)
Shopping bag containing box of "Roses" chocolates (**Ruby**)

Off stage: Tray. *On it*: white cloth (**Nurse**)
Tucker-bag containing pack of sandwiches (**Griff**)

Personal: **Ruby**: handkerchief
Nurse: stethoscope

SCENE 2

On stage: Hospital bed
Chair
Bedside cabinet. *In it*: urine bottle
Hospital paraphernalia including blood pressure gauge, thermometer, chart, et cetera

Off stage: Tray. *On it*: bandages, scissors, plaster, tweezers, paper disposal bag, et cetera (**Nurse**)

ACT II

Re-set: Two corridor chairs
Coffee machine
Hospital bed
Bedside cabinet
Hospital room chair
Hospital paraphernalia
Griff's bag

Off stage: Tray. *On it*: pills, small container of water (**Nurse**)
Two cups of coffee (**Griff**)
Wheelchair (**Nurse**)

Personal: **Rita**: cigarettes, purse containing change
Griff: handkerchief, change
Vernon: handkerchief, change

LIGHTING PLOT

Practical fittings required: nil
Two interiors — corridor, hospital room; composite setting combining the two

ACT I, Scene 1

To open: Darkness

Cue 1	When ready *Dim house lights to black-out*	(Page 1)
Cue 2	Sound of car crash *Bring up general interior lights on corridor*	(Page 1)
Cue 3	**Griff** looks towards **Nigel**'s room. Pause *Fade lights to black-out*	(Page 17)

ACT I, Scene 2

To open: Darkness

Cue 4	When ready *Bring up general interior light on room set*	(Page 18)
Cue 5	**Ruby** stands and looks agog *Black-out*	(Page 36)

ACT II

To open: Darkness

Cue 6	As cross-fade in music takes place *Bring up general interior lights on set*	(Page 37)

EFFECTS PLOT

ACT I

Cue 1	As audience is entering *Traffic noise*	(Page 1)
Cue 2	House lights fade to Black-out *The sound of a car crash*	(Page 1)
Cue 3	Black-out *Shirley Bassey sings "As Long As He Needs Me"*	(Page 17)
Cue 4	As Scene 2 begins *Fade music*	(Page18)
Cue 5	**Nigel:** " ... it's showtime!" *Shirley Bassey sings "I Am What I Am"*	(Page 36)

ACT II

Cue 6	To open Act II *Shirley Bassey sings "I Am What I Am".* *(See stage directions p. 37)*	(Page 37)
Cue 7	**The Nurse** winks and leaves *Music*	(Page 74)

A licence issued by Samuel French Ltd to perform this play does not include permission to use the Incidental music specified in this copy. Where the place of performance is already licensed by the PERFORMING RIGHT SOCIETY a return of the music used must be made to them. If the place of performance is not so licensed then application should be made to the Performing Right Society, 29 Berners Street, London W1.

A separate and additional licence from PHONOGRAPHIC PERFORMANCES LTD, Ganton House, Ganton Street, London W1 is needed whenever commercial recordings are used.

www.ingramcontent.com/pod-product-compliance
Lightning Source LLC
LaVergne TN
LVHW051758080426
835511LV00018B/3345